Materials

A Sourcebook for Walls and Floors

Francesca Torre

Materials

A Sourcebook for Walls and Floors

Photographs by
Olivier Hallot

Stewart, Tabori & Chang
New York

Contents

Introduction

There are a thousand ways to cover walls and floors. Just by changing its color, you can give a room an entirely different style. But you can also reinvent it with contemporary materials and textures, whether naturally or industrially produced, and do so in a way that reflects your own particular sensibility. This book offers resourceful do-it-yourselfers a range of simple ideas to help you figure out how to get started, fix minor defects, or completely re-envision your space.

All the materials discussed in this book—wood, paint, metal, concrete, wallpaper, and more—are evolving in ways that complement our modern style of living. Among these, natural or tinted concrete, which can be used on both floors and walls, is a highly versatile material that is being seen in an expanding variety of applications. Wood, a timeless and classic material, remains a favorite floor covering. With its distinctively authentic, natural quality, it needs no adornment. Yet contemporary applications of wood in contrasting veins, unusual finishes, or alternating light and dark strips can create dynamic visual effects that are a far cry from the monotony of the traditional hardwood floor.

Less expensive and easier to maintain, laminated floors are especially well suited for renovations because of the thinness of the material and the simplicity of insallation. Increasingly realistic designs—with raised textures, for example, that imitate wood grain so well that they are hard to distinguish from real hardwood floors—make laminates an ever more appealing alternative. Floor coverings made of vegetable fibers blend natural origins with the suppleness, quiet, and comfort of wall-to-wall carpeting; while wool, a natural fiber found mostly in the form of woven carpets, has an incomparable softness and feel. Resilient flooring, always popular for its affordability, ease of installation, and trouble-free maintenance, has even more to offer now that it is available in a wide range of designs like imitation pebbles set in surfaces of imitation ceramic. Wall coverings, too, are becoming more and more innovative, with original new wallpaper patterns, adhesive stickers, and even digital-photography prints, which can transform entire walls into giant murals.

All things considered, a comprehensive survey of the latest materials and trends in decorating walls and floors is overdue, to say the least. And this book, with its myriad suggestions, abundant illustrations, and helpful resources, is an invitation to anyone who appreciates clever and unusual solutions to create the living space that suits them best—and to do so with absolute freedom.

Concrete

Concrete, as an element with its own distinctive finish, is a great material for floors and walls because itoffers a broad palette of interesting tints and textures that are both aesthetically pleasing and easy to maintain.

As developed in 1818 by Louis Vicat, concrete is a mixture of cement, water, sand, and gravel. It has been reinvented a number of times, and today its form and appearance can be adapted to the most daring visions of architects and designers. As a composite, it has an astonishing range of options, which are achieved based on the proportions of the various components.

In the **living room**, concrete can be smoothed to a polished surface, adding a sophisticated (and not at all industrial) sheen to the space. It goes brilliantly with furniture of all kinds, whether simple or ultra-modern, and can enhance your environment in any number of ways.

In the **bathroom**, you can create special features with concrete, such as tub surrounds, surfaces around basins, and even shelves.

Concrete also goes well in the **kitchen**, for working surfaces, sinks, shelves, storage areas, and floors. Just as in the bathroom, this material must withstand the constant exposure to water, stains, and powerful cleaning agents, so it's a good idea to use reliable waterproofing films and waxes. Special casting molds can be used to make such items as concrete basins inspired by original stone ones, but because they need to be totally watertight, this kind of work is best left to professionals.

[**Tinted** Concrete]

Concrete can be colored by adding either natural or synthetic pigments. Natural pigments come from metal oxides (iron, titanium, chrome, cobalt, or magnesium), which yield subtler tints than those made with chemical colorants and are longer lasting. Mixed with the dry concrete before water is added, pigments should never comprise more than 5 percent of the total weight of the concrete mix.

You can also paint concrete surfaces with special floor paint designed for that purpose.

Smooth Concrete Surfaces

The surface of concrete can be rough or smooth. The smoother the effect you are going for, the harder it is to get right, because the smallest defect or variation will be very apparent. The surface is smoothed by drawing a straight edge sideways across the concrete, after which it can be treated in various ways to produce the final effect.

Polished concrete requires a heavy-duty polishing machine equipped with progressively finer grits of sanding disks that are used to gradually grind down the surface. Almost any structurally sound concrete floor—new or old—can be polished. After three sandings, the surface becomes smooth and shiny; if you stop sanding earlier, the floor will be smooth but with a matte finish.

To create a **waxed concrete** surface, liquid concrete mixed with colored quartz and/or surface colorants is poured onto an existing floor. It is then smoothed off with a mortarboard, plasterer's knife, or steel trowel. After the concrete has dried, the "wax" effect is produced by applying a filler followed by acrylic wax. These surfaces are easily maintained by mopping with a wax emulsion diluted with water.

Rough Concrete Surfaces

Rough surfaces are created in concrete with a small metal rolling tool applied after the material has been polished but before it has completely dried. The relief points or patterns formed by the tool give the surface the desired texture. Concrete can also be brushed to achieve a scored surface.

Once concrete is poured into the wooden casting mold, lining the inside of the mold with polyurethane film will leave the finished concrete with a glassy, varnished-looking surface. Maintain the shine by applying wax or varnish.

Previous page: Concrete, whether polished, smooth, tinted, or rough, offers an amazingly wide range of textures and colors.

Opposite: A sculptured wall panel in anthracite gray concrete with integrated shelves (by Francesco Passaniti).

Below:

High-performance concrete (HPC) can be used to make furniture that is suitable for any room in the house. These pieces are by Francesco Passaniti.

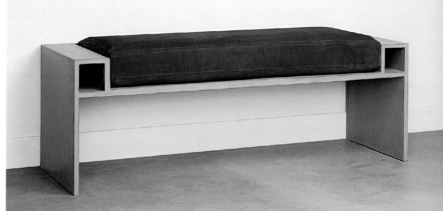

Above:

A bathtub with the purest of lines (by Francesco Passaniti) on a cowhide-patterned concrete floor. Concrete is becoming a

familiar feature of the modern bathroom.

[**Natural** Concrete]

The final shade of natural concrete depends on its components. Whether the color of the concrete is gray or white is determined by how the cement is mixed with the aggregates and finer sand.

Gray concrete continues to change once it has been laid; the color evolves over time as a result of the iron oxide it contains. This change in color can be lessened, if desired, by carefully gauging the proportions of aggregates and sand. White concrete, on the other hand, which contains no iron oxide, changes little in the long term.

The laying of a concrete floor requires expert knowledge and skill because of the complex techniques that are used, but it is quite possible to complete the finishing processes yourself. These involve four different stages.

Regardless of what finish you choose, you should be aware that it is absolutely essential for the concrete to dry entirely. Because you want the concrete to retain all its physical properties and a beautiful, long-lasting surface, it should be laid and allowed to dry under the optimum conditions recommended by the manufacturer of the cement mix you are using. If the drying process is too rapid, it will result in shrinkage, fissuring, or milky-looking grout, which will jeopardize its quality. Special products can be sprayed on the fresh concrete surface to slow down the evaporation of the water.

After drying, the first step is to spread a pigmented hardening agent over the fresh concrete to reduce its porosity and increase the hardness of the material. Allow the hardening agent to dry completely.

The next stage is to add a patina. A patina, which is sprayed on, is made up of acid metallic salts that eat into the surface of the concrete very slightly and impregnate it with extra color. This can produce an aged or marbled appearance, as you wish.

Next is a fixative, applied with a roller, that "seals" the concrete, hardening the surface even more and enabling wax to adhere to it more effectively. Take care to ensure that the layer of fixative is sufficiently thick and regular, and that it dries completely. You can test this by passing a wet sponge over the surface. The waterproofing effect should be obvious everywhere, with no remaining absorbent patches.

Once you have checked this to your satisfaction, the wax can be applied. Wax functions as a hard-wearing sealer and gives the surface a slightly shiny appearance that will highlight the tint of the hardening agent and patina. When the wax is dry, it will protect the floor from stains and blemishes. The floor can be treated just like a hardwood floor, with wax being applied at intervals to maintain its luster.

Fiber-Reinforced Concrete

Concrete reinforced with sisal, made up of hemp stalk shavings and 85 percent hydraulic lime, is a sound and dry material for walls.

Reinforced concrete can be found in many types of components, including slabs, beams, columns, and more. These blocks are designed to include grooves and holes through which electrical wires and water pipes can be passed. The thermal efficiency of this material, which does not require any complementary insulating material, is a major energy saver. Because it is natural, it should be covered with a simple lime finish, which allows it to breathe. In terms of cost, reinforced concrete is more economical than ordinary concrete.

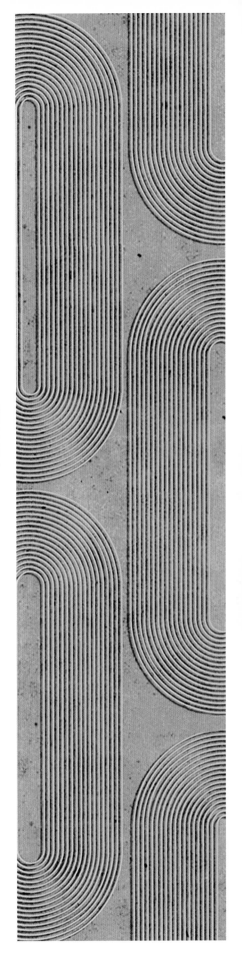

[Finishes]

After concrete has dried (allow one day per ½ inch [1 cm] of thickness), the patina is sprayed on and spread with a circular motion, using a nylon brush with a long handle like a deck scrubber. A thorough cleaning will remove any excess. The fixative is then applied in two uniform layers to the wet floor, using a roller with short bristles. Use 4 cups for every 80 to 100 square feet (1 liter for every 8 to 10 square meters).

The wax is applied with a roller, in two layers. Apply one layer lengthwise and the second layer widthwise 4 to 6 hours after the first. To obtain a moiré effect, the surface can be very lightly sanded.

Above:

Japanese-style, set with mirror fragments, or stonelike, concrete can be adapted to any style and any need.

Right:

Le Dean Burrus, specialists in the use of concrete, perfected a decorative wall covering with geometric motifs that can be used for both interiors and exteriors.

Limewash

Lime is a **natural binding agent** that is ideal for applying to brick, stone, or concrete. It is very easy to work with, adhering well to all these natural surfaces. For any other type of surface, it needs to be mixed with vinyl glue or some kind of acrylic binder diluted with water. Dry, resistant to wear, and inexpensive, lime also possesses a structural flexibility that allows it to withstand sudden changes of temperature without cracking or fissuring. Unused lime can be kept indefinitely in a closed container, so if you buy too much, it won't be wasted. Lime is also highly absorbent, with **disinfectant and fungicidal properties.** Thanks to its excellent compatibility with natural materials, lime can be readily mixed with many different coloring agents.

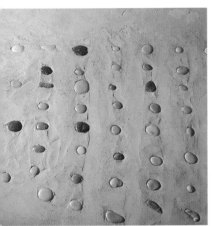

[**Plasterer's** Knife]

You can obtain a smooth lime finish by using a broad plasterer's knife. But take care that the lime is applied with a uniform thickness or you will need to go back over it with a sander once it is dry. On the other hand, if you have any thin spots, you can always add more. If the knife leaves a wrinkle on the surface, you can rub it off when the lime is dry.

Painting a Wall with Limewash

First, prepare the surface by applying any generic wall covering, available at home improvement stores and hardware stores. Choose one with more or less relief, according to the texture you want.

Next, apply three layers of limewash with a graining brush, allowing each layer 24 hours to dry. For convenience, choose ready-to-use lime paste and dilute it with 3 parts water, using a mixer or an electric drill fitted with a paint mixer head. This limewash solution, without pigments, is virtually transparent—which is why you need several thin layers to achieve the desired effect.

Tinting Limewash

Dilute pigment powder (the quantity of pigment used should not exceed 20 percent of the weight of the lime) in a little water to make a smooth paste; add a drop of liquid soap or alcohol to facilitate the distribution of the pigment throughout the water. Stir this mixture into the lime solution, taking special care to note the exact quantities used so you can duplicate the colors accurately, if necessary. Then apply the finished limewash to walls, using a broad paintbrush.

Opposite:
Lime-washed walls with a mix of calcined ocher, lightened with white to produce a delicately nuanced, powdery covering.

Below:
To apply a lime finish, you can use a wallpaper brush (working up and down and side to side). The final layer will soften the effects of the brush, leaving a subtle finish.

Tadelakt

The intensity of the color diminishes as it dries, and for this reason, several coats are necessary. For a cloudy effect, paint on the limewash with a graining brush, then dab with a sponge or cloth. The same powdery effect can be achieved with a casein distemper (casein is a phosphoprotein of milk), which has some distinctive characteristics: It covers surfaces very well, is extremely matte in appearance, and absorbs colors to perfection.

There are a number of Web sites that allow you to visualize how your painting project is likely to turn out, and some have online color-consultant services.

Tadelakt is an especially pure form of lime found in Morocco, and the stucco technique of applying it is closely associated with the city of Marrakesh. The lime is first sifted, then combined with a natural pigment, wetted, and carefully mixed. It is then applied to the area to be covered with a trowel, which results in a roughish surface, before being smoothed off in a thin layer. A luster is obtained by using a second mix of eggs and liquid soap (use 2 pounds [1 kilogram] of soap to 50 to 100 eggs, depending on the richness of the mix), which produces a shiny, cracked effect. At this point, the *tadelakt* is polished and hardened using stones or abrasives that are harder than the plaster finish. This mechanical polishing, inch by inch, is what gives *tadelakt* its final, smooth effect.

Opposite:
The waterproof qualities of *tadelakt* make it the ideal choice for showers and bathrooms.

[**Walls** and Waterproofing]

Tadelakt can be applied to solidly constructed concrete, brick, or stone walls as well as to nearly all other irregular surfaces with a base of lime, cement, and sand. The liquid soap treatment is what makes the material waterproof, and this must be applied correctly on the initial mix, using a cloth, within 24 hours of laying.

One person working alone cannot do more than 30 to 40 square feet (3 to 4 square meters) per day. If you are planning to line a large area with *tadelakt,* you will need two or more workers to help you.

Tadelakt has a waterproofing effect, and its smooth texture allows condensation to run off the walls. It is therefore a useful material in bathrooms, kitchens, and other areas that are likely to get wet. Greatly appreciated for its durability and wide variety of colors, *tadelakt* can also be used for living rooms and bedrooms.

Ready-to-use mixes exist on the market that produce very similar effects in a wide range of colors. You can learn the authentic *tadelakt* technique by taking a class or buying a how-to CD along with a product that is very similar to *tadelakt* and is inexpensive and easy to apply.

It takes four months for *tadelakt* to cure and reach the appropriate degree of hardness, and it is crucial to allow this time to elapse when applying it in bathrooms or showers. In the first two months of drying, it is all-important to protect the *tadelakt,* given that its finished hardness develops so slowly.

Above:

Lime finishes are both sound and aesthetically pleasing; they can be brushed, finished with a knife, or smoothed by hand. Their velvety appearance changes with the light.

Opposite:

A coffee-colored finish blends in perfect harmony with the darker sheen of wood.

Maintaining Tadelakt

To keep *tadelakt* in good condition, wash it with soft, natural soap like olive-oil or black soaps; never use scouring creams or products designed to attack lime deposits. *Tadelakt* around bathtubs and sinks that are used frequently should be greased with natural soap once a month.

Paint

Paint of any kind is basically made up of resin, or binder, which assists the formation of the film of paint and gives it its chief properties; pigments and fillers, which provide opacity and color; solvents such as water or turpentine, which help achieve the proper viscosity; and special additives such as anti-fungal solutions.

Several trends in the use of paint for decoration have emerged in recent years, the following among them:

- A heightened interest in **contrasts** as a resolutely contemporary way of organizing living space: broad surfaces of vivid colors, multicolored stenciled motifs, and furnishings revived with vibrant fresh paint.
- Embracing **minimalism** without starkness. The Scandinavian style exemplifies this trend toward simplicity and refinement. Rooms filled with sensual, unembellished shapes offer a harmony and balance of their own. Quality materials and natural colors are the main ingredients of these calm, light-filled, welcoming interiors.
- A new interest in polar themes and poetic hues of blue, along with delicate cameos of white, producing an ambiance of quiet **serenity**.
- A taste for the downright eccentric and **theatrical**. Here the idea is to put together carefully selected, opulent accessories—such as huge chandeliers and rich fabrics—matched by deep luscious colors, with the primary goal of creating unusual spaces.

Oil-Based Paints

Oil-based paints have always been popular because of their excellent coverage and extreme durability. Their hard film, which is both smooth and perfectly adhesive, allows them to be used in humid rooms, where a shiny veneer is often preferred. But oil-based paints are becoming limited in availabilty due to their high VOC (volatile organic component) content, which is known to be hazardous to human health. They are also less convenient to work with than water-based paints; are diluted and cleaned up with turpentine or white spirit, which have an unpleasant smell (although this can be avoided by using the newer odorless form of spirit); and have a tendency to turn yellow with age. A new generation of oil-based paints is available now. Unlike traditional ones, which take 72 hours to dry, they take between 4 and 12 hours, depending on the brand. Another advantage of the new oil paints is that their solvent content is less than half that of their traditional counterparts, which makes them correspondingly less dangerous to human health and the environment.

The New Generation of Latex Paints

New latex and acrylic paints, which consist of alkyd or synthetic resin in a single-coat emulsion, have a remarkable covering capacity that gives them the toughness of traditional oil-based paints without the disadvantages (yellowing, extended drying time, smell). They come in a glossy finish, offering the same sheen as oil paints—but with only one coat. In addition, latex paint is now offered in low or no-VOC composition, making it healthier for the home and the environment.

The matte version of latex paint is soft and subtle, but also washable and stain-resistant. It dries quickly; it is also totally odorless and contains very few VOCs. Its thoroughly modern colors are derived from very high-quality mineral and organic components.

Acrylic Paints

Acrylics are composed of synthetic polymers; they are extremely versatile as well as water-soluble, and form an impermeable film when dry. Their resistance to wear and tear and their general longevity are close to those of oil-based paints. These water-based products outperform all others in sales on the interior decoration market. Their drying time of 30 minutes means that you don't have to wait long between coats, and clean-up is easy, with soap and water. Acrylic paints are nonpolluting, almost odorless, nonflammable, and washable. Acrylics adhere well to every kind of surface and can be applied in humid areas such as kitchens and baths as well as in living rooms and bedrooms. Acrylics have a high resistance to scoring, scratching, cracking, and yellowing. But beware: They must be applied in a single session. You cannot paint wet alongside an area that has already dried, because the line where you started later and the brushstrokes will be painfully visible.

Opposite:
The use of several shades of orange creates an atmosphere of softness and warmth in a living room.

Above:
Lively colors give a touch of playfulness to a dining area.

Fashionable stripes are
not only decorative but
also useful for visually
modifying irregularities
in a space.

Silky semi-gloss paints
can be used in any room
in the house.

Above and below:

Poetic motifs and subtle shadings give life to wall surfaces.

Paint Finishes

The quality of the finish depends on the preparation of the wall or surface you are painting. An environmentally friendly alternative to oil finishes are water-based ones, which can easily be wiped or washed clean.

Matte finish has a powdery appearance that can mask many small imperfections in the surface underneath. Matte paints are most suitable for ceilings, hallways, and bedrooms.

Semi-gloss finish offers a silky, warm look. It is excellent for bedrooms and living rooms as well as wainscoting and other wood details.

Gloss finish is easy to clean and impervious to moisture. It is best for kitchens and bathrooms but may also be used to highlight doors and windows in rooms that are otherwise painted with a semi-gloss finish.

Eggshell finish is ideal for woodwork, with a pleasant, subtle sheen. Oil-based eggshell is a highly durable standard that is even suitable for radiators.

Preparing Paint Surfaces

Most surfaces need to be properly prepared to facilitate the application of paint. A thorough cleaning and the elimination of stains are important: Any dirt, grease marks, or dust can prevent the paint from adhering.

Remove all the contents of the room, vacuum the floors well, inspect the surfaces to be painted, and identify places where the plaster or other surface needs repair. Before you begin, make sure the floor is fully protected with a dropcloth or plastic sheeting.

Sponge all the surfaces to be painted with a solution of laundry detergent and water; this will clean and prepare the surface as well as eliminate traces of grease or nicotine stains. After cleaning, rinse the surfaces with a sponge dipped in clean water.

Steam cleaning can also be effective on exceptionally dirty surfaces, but it may prevent the paint from adhering well. If you steam clean the surface, sand the surface after it is completely dry and before you begin painting. After sanding, vacuum again and wipe the walls with a damp sponge.

Holes and cracks should be enlarged with a metal trowel or putty knife, then patched with a spackling compound, ready-made or mixed with water.

If the room you are painting has wallpaper on the walls, you can paint over the paper or remove it. To remove it, apply water to the walls with a sponge or sprayer. Allow time for the wallpaper to absorb the water, then remove it with a trowel or spatula. The paper should come off easily; if it doesn't, soak it with more water. A quicker way is to use a steam remover to unglue the wallpaper. (These can be rented at paint stores and home improvement stores.) Set

Opposite:

If a wall space is not divided in different colors, the ceiling height is accentuated.

Above:

Rich fabrics echo the matte color of the wall, creating a decorative untity.

Left:

A natural ambiance of pale wood and soft, sandy tones predominates in this passageway.

the steam remover against the wall, allowing the steam to penetrate the paper, then skin it off with a spatula, taking care not to damage the wall surface.

If the plasterwork is old, everything covering it should be removed with a brush. Should the surface be damaged nevertheless, reinforce it with a patching plaster. The same goes for new plaster, which will totally absorb the first coat of paint.

On wood that has several coats of paint already, use a chemical paint remover to get down to the original surface.

To remove both varnish and paint, or to polish an irregular surface, use a sander. To smooth off a wall or ceiling, first rub by hand with coarse sandpaper, then rub with a finer-grain paper to give a smooth surface.

Remove the surface dust with a soft brush or damp cloth, then apply a first coat of paint diluted with 5 to 10 percent water. This basecoat will diminish the absorbency of the surface and improve the paint's adherence.

Above:

Delicate designs and stripes can be used to enliven any wall.

[**Paint** and Cleanliness]

Some types of paint have a definite impact on domestic hygiene. Some paints contain a substance that kills dust mites, which is effective for a number of years; they also prevent the development of the mildew on which mites feed. Insecticide paints deter undesirable insects, most of them for at least three years. A recent innovation is bactericide paint, which can help protect the house from pathogenic bacteria such as salmonella, streptococcus, and staphylococcus.

For major sanding work on wooden floors, walls, doors, or other areas, use a circular electric sander. Take care to use the same pressure everywhere and replace the sandpaper frequently so the result will be uniform. Don't forget that it is essential to wear a dust mask when working with an electric sander.

Choice of Colors

Warm tints lend a touch of gaiety to north-facing rooms that are well-lit but do not receive direct sunlight. These colors belong to the range of reds, oranges, yellows, pinks, ochers, and browns. Applied in small touches, they create an ambiance of warmth and vitality.

The cooler tints—blues, violets, and greens—produce a sense of space and a mood of relaxation. Gray, which is becoming ever more popular, is most elegant and refined in a matte or satin finish. It can be warmed up with one- or two-color additions, but the rule of thumb is not to use more than three colors in the same room, always respecting the following proportions: 80 percent for the dominant tint; 15 percent and 5 percent, respectively, for the second and third colors.

White is a safe choice if you are not sure of what colors to use. It emphasizes the qualities of furniture, floors, and fabric. For a soft effect, matte is the best finish; subtle and gentle, it also masks—to some extent—irregularities in the surface. By contrast,

a warm, silky, semi-gloss finish will serve for living areas and decorative wooden features such as moldings and baseboards.

Shiny, full-gloss paint heightens its own color and is especially suitable for bathrooms and showers.

Instead of strong contrasting colors, choose subtler ones that vary between light and dark, matte and semi-gloss, or rough and smooth surfaces so that one tint ends up more strongly present than another in a given space. If in doubt, refer to the color charts in the paint store or home improvement store, on many design Web sites, or create your own chart using paint samples you can buy in small quantities.

By painting the lower wall sections (generally the lower third of the wall space) in darker tones, contrasting them with a light shade above, you can attract the eye away from the ceiling.

Stripes are also popular and are highly decorative. They create optical illusions that make it possible to visually correct irregularities. For example, when stripes run up vertically from the floor, they give an impression of height, and when they run horizontal, they can make a too-high ceiling seem more balanced.

Using the Right Brushes

For walls, ceilings, or any other very large surface, use 4- to 6-inch (100- to 150-mm) brushes; for narrow edges, such as moldings, use 1- to 2-inch (25- to 50-mm) brushes. Large, flat surfaces like doors and shelves require 2- to 3-inch (50- to 75-mm) brushes. The best size brush for narrow wood surfaces like windowsills and doorframes is 1 to 1½ inches (25 to 40 mm).

Above:

"Méchants oiseaux," a hand-painted pattern, created by craftsmen at Emery & Cie.

Opposite:

Emery & Cie's "Méchants oiseaux" in gray, on muslin curtains, in a room painted blue-gray.

Changing the Balance

Paint allows you to correct perspectives and bring balance to rooms with less-than-perfect dimensions. For example, to bring together a room that is longer than it is wide, with a very high ceiling, you might paint the ceiling and the upper third of the walls in a deep color like brick red. By dividing up wall surfaces, you can reduce a sense of disproportionate height even further.

Wallpaper

Colors, patterns, textures—wallpaper offers an incredibly wide choice of all three. This traditional wall covering has made something of a comeback with fresh new collections by respected designers. A versatile product that is just as suitable for contemporary décor as for more classic ones, wallpaper can add a touch of modernity to an atmosphere that might otherwise be a little dated, or a hint of nostalgia to a recently built apartment. It makes walls look neat, dynamic, and decorative. And once you know how to do it, wallpaper can be hung easily and quickly. It takes much less time to paper a room than to paint it. If you account for drying time between coats, painting a room can take several days, whereas wallpapering the average room seldom takes more than 12 hours if the walls are properly prepared.

Whether it is **hand-painted, solid-colored, patterned, smooth, textured, geometric, retro, or contemporary,** wallpaper is a decorative element that can be adapted to every taste and budget. Made from a variety of materials, including paper, fabric, and substances such as glass, sand, and natural fibers, wallpaper offers vast choices. Some wallpaper is plain white, to be painted later, and is best suited for unplastered walls with cracks in them that need to be masked. Whatever its purpose, before buying wallpaper it is important to have a clear idea about the type of covering you want and how you intend to install it.

For those who expect to redecorate a room within a few years (you may tire of a given décor quickly, or perhaps you have children who will grow out of it), the best choice is wallpaper that can be easily removed. Wallpapers coated with a layer of vinyl, for example, are much harder to remove than those with a plain paper surface.

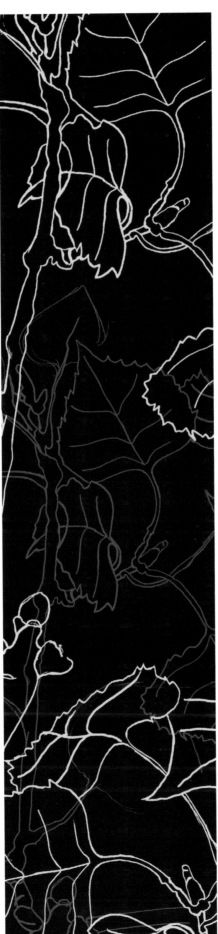

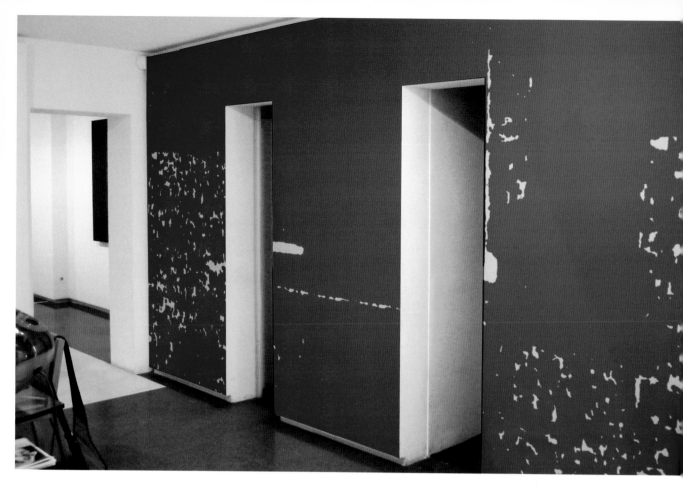

Above, right, and opposite:

Specialty shops are now producing trendy personalized wall coverings in small quantities. They also offer collections created by designers that include a wide range of colors, sizes, and paper qualities.

Textured Wallpapers

There is an infinite choice of textures that are ideal both for masking surface defects and for imitating materials like plaster, wood, and textiles.

To camouflage a cracked plaster wall, grass or bamboo wallpapers are the most ecologically sound solution, along with wallpapers made entirely of recycled paper and wood shavings, with no color additives.

Lincrusta, a hard-wearing waterproof paper, has a texture that is very close to that of linoleum. It calls for extra-strong glue and is usually found in home improvement stores with the imitation wood and plaster products.

Flocked wallpapers, made by gluing very short textile fibers to the surface of the paper, offer a convincing imitation of luxurious fabrics.

Embossed vinyl wallpapers are specially treated during the manufacturing process so that their surfaces imitate stone, tiles, and even the weave of textiles. Because of its thickness, this wallpaper can be glued to bare brick and other irregular wall surfaces.

Foil Wallpapers

Foil wallpapers consist of metallic plastic film adhered to a paper backing. This type of paper can be difficult to work with; it can be unforgiving if it gets wrinkled or folded and has a tendency to reveal any defects in the wall behind it.

The Art of Hanging Wallpaper

Measure the first strip on the wall, leaving a margin of 2 inches (5 cm) at the top and bottom. Mark it with a pencil for cutting. Use this first strip as a template for cutting several strips at a time; then spread the back of each length of paper with glue and apply them one by one to the wall, taking care that the patterns match up exactly. When applying the glue, place a glob in the middle of each strip and brush it out to the edges. Do not allow dirt or grit to get into the glue bucket, and keep your gluing table clean, carefully wiping off glue splashes as they occur. You can also use the sides of the table to align the paper. To allow the glue to penetrate the paper and to keep it from drying out, loosely fold the paper back to back without flattening the folds. This will give it a chance to absorb the glue and relax. Some pre-glued ready-to-hang wallpapers may need a similar period for absorption.

Before hanging the first strip, draw a vertical line on the wall using a level. This very simple maneuver is vital for achieving a successful result. Handle the wallpaper with great care as you slide the first strip gently into place, butting it against the vertical line. Use your palms to press the paper onto the wall. Using a clean, dry brush, brush the strips flat against the wall from the center outward to remove bubbles and smooth the paper into position. Last, double-check the vertical alignment with the level.

It is now possible to re-create an old wallpaper pattern using the computer. You can measure it, reproduce its colors with precision, and print enough of the paper (with or without modifications of your own) to cover the surface you are working with.

Below: Decorative stickers are easy to apply and come in a variety of large and small designs.

Decorative Stickers

The fashion for decorative stickers has spawned a quantity of Web sites that offer innumerable designs in different colors and sizes: oversized flowers or stones, trees, coral, and even motifs from the seventies and other eras.

Applying Decorative Stickers

The wall needs to be dry, clean, and smooth, and there should be no heater nearby. Keep the sticker at room temperature for 24 hours before you apply it. If the wall has slight bumps or cavities, or is surface-coated with vinyl, test it for adhesion with a snippet of the sticker.

Cut out the sticker, leaving an ample margin around the design. Carefully remove the protective film and place the sticker where you want it. Push out any air bubbles by firmly pressing sideways with a soft, dry cloth toward the edges of the sticker.

Wall Fabric

There is a vast choice of textile wall coverings available on the market, of every possible texture and quality, to harmonize with any decorative style. Among those offered are **solid-colored or striped** velvet, silks in designs that are both resolutely modern and representative of the past, and **stain-resistant, UV-resistant, and flame-resistant** fabrics that were originally manufactured for hotels, schools, and public buildings, but are now being manufactured for residential use.

In addition, there are plenty of contemporary textiles with specific **textural** or **material effects** produced through modern technology. Manufacturers, working to order, use every possible weaving technique, ancient or modern, to turn out **contemporary creations as well as reproductions** taken from archives and records of past designs.

Types of Wall Fabric

There are two main types of textile products for covering walls: actual fabrics, which are complicated to put in place, and wall covering that looks like fabric but is pre-glued to a backing, making it as easy to hang as wallpaper.

Fabrics

Most upholstery fabrics for furniture—whether cotton, linen, or wool—can be stretched onto a wall. They are often mixed with synthetic fibers, which strengthens them and ensures that they last. Some are flame-resistant and treated against both everyday stains and the slow discoloration caused by ultraviolet rays.

Pre-Glued Textiles

The pre-glued textiles are much harder-wearing than plain fabrics. In addition to their fire-, stain- and UV-resistant qualities, they can be washed and even scrubbed. To calculate the quantity of fabric you will need, take the room's dimensions and add 4 inches (10 cm) to the height and width before cutting out the panel.

Stretching Fabrics

Glue wooden moldings around the periphery of the wall. Staple felt to the wall and against the moldings. Starting from the top, fix the fabric in position with a few staples. Then set staples every 4 inches (10 cm), moving outward from the center.

When the first wall is covered, the fabric will overflow 4 inches (10 cm) onto the adjoining wall. Thereafter, use wall guards, such as corner guards or handrails, stapling a strip of cardboard 1 inch (2 cm) wide inside the fabric. In this way, you can achieve neat angles while concealing the staples.

Opposite and right:
Most furniture upholstery fabrics, whether classic or contemporary in style, can be stretched onto walls. They often have fire-, stain-, and UV-resistant properties and are usually easy to clean as well.

Carpet

Wall-to-wall carpeting may have been considered unfashionable in recent years, but it remains the most widely used floor covering, especially in apartments. **Woven, tufted, or felted**, in wool, synthetic fiber, or a mixture of the two, wall-to-wall carpeting is unrivaled in creating a quiet, cozy environment. It comes in a rainbow of colors and patterns, can be matched to any style of furnishings, and often serves as the starting point for entire decorating projects. Moreover, it is **economical, durable**, and can be pretreated to resist stains and require only minimal maintenance. It invites you to go shoeless and effectively muffles all kinds of noises, absorbing the airborne sounds of televisions or musical instruments, and protecting against impact sounds like footsteps, knocks, and chairs being shifted. The thicker it is, the more useful it will be in this capacity. And finally, a carpet is a great energy-saver, being 10 to 12 times more effective than hard flooring for the retention of heat, translating to as much as a 6 percent saving on heating bills.

Contrary to the accepted wisdom, wall-to-wall carpeting is both **healthy and hygienic**. It captures dust, which can then be efficiently removed with a vacuum cleaner, and thus reduces by half the presence in the air of particles that can cause allergies. Treating carpeting with anti-stain agents can help keep floors clean and hygienic, but be careful of cetain products, like Teflon or Scotchgard, that are known to be health risks. As a general rule, good and regular cleaning coupled with a daily airing of the room will be quite enough to keep carpeting dirt-free. If you are particularly concerned about dirt and allergens, opt for a brand of carpet that has been treated against all forms of mites. The substances used for this are environmentally friendly and will also protect the carpet from mold and fungus.

The topside of the carpet, on which you walk, is called the pile. Beneath this, and just as important, is the backing. Aside from traditional **weaving techniques**, two modern manufacturing methods have helped to keep wall-to-wall carpeting affordable: needle punching and tufting. The longevity and toughness of a carpet depend on the length and density of the fibers used in its pile. A thick carpet, with a high, open pile, is very attractive to the eye and feels great underfoot; but it is best suited to places where you relax, such as the bedroom or living room. A short, tight pile will be harder wearing and more suitable for places where there is plenty of traffic (entrances and hallways) and where there is a greater likelihood of it getting stained or marked (in the dining room, for example).

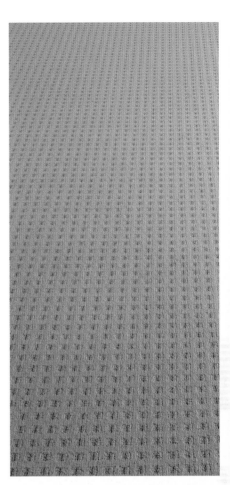

Needle-punch carpets are composed of successive layers of fiber stacked on a primary backing—which feels like felt—that is then glued on a secondary backing. If the fibers are long and held in place like this, the resulting carpet will be of high quality, with an attractive finish. If the fibers are short, the adhesive glue penetrates the entire pile and stiffens, flattens, and roughens the surface, making it scratchy to the touch and lowering the quality.

The pile of **tufted carpets** is inserted into its backing by a system of stitching combined with gluing, which makes it possible to give the product a variety of different surface appearances. These carpets come in both strips and squares and are relatively inexpensive.

A new form of wall-to-wall carpeting has come on the market—tufted carpet on a felt backing. In addition to its excellent soundproofing and heat-retaining properties, this product is incredibly comfortable to walk on.

Woven carpets are the most expensive, long-lasting, and comfortable of all. Their looped pile is manufactured at the same time as their backing on a special loom, and can be either monochrome or patterned. This traditional weaving technique is confined to wool and synthetic fibers of the highest quality.

Carpet Piles

There is a wide array of pile textures, which vary according to the way the fibers are assembled.

Loop pile: The strands form loops embedded in the backing of the carpet.

Cut pile: The strands are cut at the tips to create a silky finish.

Cut-loop pile: Some areas of the pile are looped and some areas are cut to create patterns.

Saxony pile: The thickness of the long strands in the cut pile varies between ¼ and ½ inch (8 and 12 mm) in length, which makes for a wavy effect.

Patterned pile: This surface offers two lengths of strands, which yield a texture that can be used to create reliefs and motifs.

Frieze: The strands of fiber are twisted so that their tips coil like corkscrews.

Opposite and above:
Wall-to-wall carpeting is an ideal floor covering if you are trying to create a soft, cozy, relaxing atmosphere in a room. The pile can have any number of looks, and the higher it is, the more pleasing it will be to walk on and look at.

Fibers

The choice between natural and synthetic fibers will have a direct influence on the lifespan of your carpet.

Natural Fibers

Wool has the advantage of retaining its flexibility and beauty longer than any other material. It can easily last for 20 years or more, but its cost may be prohibitive. The backing of most woven carpets is made of cotton, and the pile may also contain cotton. Hard-wearing and easy to dye, cotton can be difficult to maintain and is expensive.

Vegetable Fibers

Natural vegetable fibers come in many different textures and weaves, and they generally create a soft effect in a room. They are relatively robust and easy to maintain—as a rule, all they require is regular vacuuming.

Coconut matting, made with coconut fibers, looks fine but is harsh and scratchy to the touch. The more expensive sea grass, grown in flooded fields, has a finer, softer feel. It is also fairly resistant to stains and mites. Sisal, composed of white fibers from the American aloe plant, can be blended with wool to create herringbone, basket weave, and bouclé weaves, among other patterns.

Carpets made of vegetable fibers are decorative, hard-wearing, resistant to rot, and inexpensive. They can be used in every room in the house and are especially appropriate for dining areas. Generally backed with non-slip latex and trimmed with broad cotton edges, these carpets can be kept dust-free with a vacuum cleaner. From time to time, they should be dampened a little with a cloth or mist to tighten their knotting. The original shine of sea grass can be restored by wiping with a damp cloth.

Reducing the Environmental Footprint

The carpet industry is working to minimize their products' impact on the environment, by focusing on the three Rs—reduce, reuse, and recycle. Efforts are being made to develop methods whereby carpeting, when it reaches the end of its long life, can be reused to make new carpet or recycled into a variety of products, such as roofing shingles, railroad ties, or automotive parts.

Opposite:
Natural materials often enrich one another when intelligently blended. Beautiful woven patterns include mixed fibers like (1) artificial leather and paper, (4) paper and sea grass, or (5) sisal. Versatile fibers also include (2) hemp or (3) jute, linen, and leather.

[**Paper** Fiber]

Paper-fiber carpets have appeared on and off over the last century on the plant-fiber carpet market. Used by itself or in combination with sisal, this matte, smooth material is easy to maintain with a damp sponge. On the other hand, it is vulnerable to hot liquids because of its waxed surface. You can find both historical examples and recent designs.

2

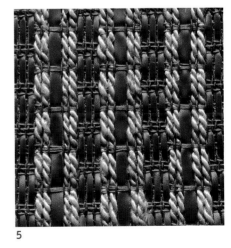

5

Synthetic Fibers

Previous spread:

In two reception areas,
a rust-colored carpet
made of hemp and jute
fibers and a slate gray
hemp carpet create a
space that is chic and
elegant.

Most carpets today are made of nylon. Used on its own or in association with other fibers, this material is highly resistant and will retain its volume for many years. Nylon can be adapted to any carpet-manufacturing process, but in every circumstance must be treated for static control.

Polyester fiber looks and feels like nylon but is not as resilient. Acrylic fibers closely resemble wool in terms of their appearance, but are not nearly as durable. Polypropylene, or olefin, fiber—the most recent addition to the synthetic options—is the least expensive but also the least robust. In most cases, it is better to opt for a carpet with a very thick pile. On the other hand, polypropylene is a good choice for a bathroom because it is resistant to water and rot.

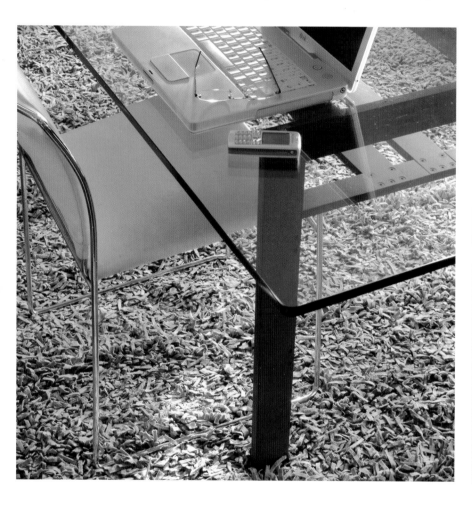

Above:

The material of a floor covering should be chosen according to its expected use and location. A carpet made of leather strips will be fine for a room that is seldom used, while carpet squares or cut-pile carpeting is best for areas that see plenty of traffic.

Colors

Carpeting in rich, deep colors will create a warm, intimate ambiance in a bedroom or office. Use light or pastel-colored carpets, preferably in one color, to give subtlety and elegance to a room while making it feel larger than it is. Patterned carpets tend to create a more personal, fanciful look.

Laying Carpets

Do-It-Yourself Laying

The simplest, quickest, and cheapest way to lay a carpet is to do it yourself—by cutting it to the correct dimensions and installing it without glue or carpet tacks. This method is best for smaller, less frequently used areas. For such applications, use a carpet with a thick, stable backing, which increases its weight. To make sure it doesn't shift, use double-stick tape around the edges. This laying method is not recommended for carpet squares.

Laying with Glue

Before you begin, make sure the floor is smooth, dry, and clean, then apply the glue, followed by the carpet. This method can be used for all kinds of carpets except traditional woven ones, and is especially suitable for large, heavily used rooms.

(For very large areas, it is best to hire a professional carpet layer.) A new kind of glue or fixative has been developed that can be applied with a roller, which hugely facilitates the process.

Laying with Stretchers

This is an expensive procedure, best left to professionals, which is essential for woven or tufted carpets with double backings. The carpet is stretched along tackless strips and in front of doors using a knee kicker and power stretcher. Using this technique, the life of the carpet is augmented by about a third; its insulating capacity and sheer comfort are also greatly improved. Another benefit of this laying technique is that it may allow you to reuse the carpet elsewhere later.

Carpet Maintenance

Preventing Crush Marks

Heavy furniture resting on a carpet should be shifted a bit from time to time to avoid permanently crushing the carpet in those spots. Also, it is an excellent idea to keep scraps trimmed from the original carpet to place under the feet of furniture items.

Prepare for Eventual Stains

Take simple protective measures, like putting mats and foot scrapers at entrances, to prevent dirt from entering the house on people's shoes.

In addition, choose a carpet that has been treated against staining, which helps keep dirt and dust from getting into the fibers and makes them easy to vacuum out. Liquids are not readily absorbed by modern carpets but stay in droplets on the surface for a short time until they can be wiped away with a cotton cloth or paper towel. To remove greasy stains, dip a clean cloth in stain remover (trichloroethylene) and dab around the stain until you reach the center, absorbing all the liquid. Repeat, if necessary.

Ordinary Maintenance

Vacuum the carpet at least twice a week to keep it in good condition.

Wood

Wood is a **noble** material; it warms the atmosphere of a home like nothing else. Oak, chestnut, and pine of different species have been popular for time immemorial, but today people are increasingly using other varieties of wood grown both at home and abroad—notably darker-colored species—which offer a **wide range of looks and tints**.

With their tongue-and-groove assembly and easy fastening, wooden floorboards are just as good for brand-new construction as for renovating an older living room or bedroom, whatever the original floor.

Laminate floors are quickly installed, and whether they consist of one layer or several, they will always combine economy with refinement, on account of their natural longevity. To break the monotony of traditional hardwood floors, try mixing species and floorboards of different lengths.

Hardwood Floors

Hardwood floors are authentically natural, beautiful, and inviting; they add a note of elegant living to any room. They offer a wide aesthetic choice with many different types of finishes and many distinct ways of arranging the boards.

Wood has thousands of different tints, ranging from white beech to the dark brown of chestnut and the red of merbau. Iroko, wenge, pine, and teak all vary widely in board width and finish, but only those varieties of wood selected for their hardness and density should be used for flooring. A good hardwood floor should last at least 70 years, which makes it by far the cheapest floor available.

There are basically two types of hardwood floor in use today: solid wood and engineered wood.

Solid Wood

Solid wood floors are generally made of 1-inch-thick (25 mm) floorboards, delivered in their natural state. They are sanded and varnished after they have been laid. Tongue-and-groove floorboards are nailed to joists, a process that effectively raises the floor level by at least 3 inches (7 cm). This may not be ideal for renovation purposes, but it is popular in new construction and in the restoration of old hardwood flooring. For practical reasons, manufacturers have begun to offer thinner boards, between ¼ and ¾ inch (8 and 20 mm) thick. These are intended to be nailed down, but if they are less than ½ inch (12 mm) thick, they can also be glued.

Preceding page:

Whether it is new or reclaimed hardwood, wood flooring has authenticity, refinement, and durability. The best places for it are living rooms, dining rooms, and bedrooms, but exotic wood or bamboo will also suit kitchens and bathrooms. Before making your choice, note the conditions inherent to each room: heavy traffic, especially in and out of the house, or the risk of food stains will dictate which wood you need.

Opposite:

The tint, width, and placement of floorboards should be carefully studied, keeping in mind that you want the wood to harmonize well with the elements already present in your home—the furniture, existing wood features, and wall colors.

[Reclaimed Hardwood Floors]

If you are looking for old wooden floorboards with a good patina for a restoration project, antiques dealers who specialize in salvaging old building materials often have them in stock. There are several companies, some conveniently found online, that only sell hardwood flooring.

[**Retified** Wood]

Retified wood is a modern European treatment for local species that subjects the wood to very high temperatures. No chemical substance is added, and the physical properties of the wood are heavily reinforced—notably its resistance to water, dimensional stability, surface hardness, and resistance to rot.

Heat-Treated Wood

One of the processes used since the 1990s in France and Europe consists of subjecting wood to heat treatment ranging from approximately 350° to 480°F (180° to 250°C)—depending on parameters such as atmosphere, temperature, processing time, rate of heating, species, weight and dimension of the pieces, and original moisture of the wood. The result is a rearrangement of the wood's molecular structure, causing it to turn brown and become harder and more stable; it can also be immediately planed, in bulk. The thermal treatment brings about a clear improvement in durability: a noticeable reduction in moisture absorption and the elimination of some of the nutrients required by wood-rotting fungi.

The treatment works for all types of wood, from poplar, ash, and beech right through to the various species of pine. Moreover, it is thoroughly ecological because it produces no toxic side-effects for the environment.

Engineered Wood

Engineered wood, also called composite wood, which is scarcely thicker than the average carpet, is a contemporary material that can re-create the warmth and charm of an old floor. It is manufactured by binding wood strands, particles, fibers, or veneers together with adhesives. A surface layer of solid wood is glued to the composite core layer, which in turn is glued to a counterbalancing layer of wood. This bottom layer may also be covered with adhesive polyurethane foam. The strip self-adheres when put in place.

Engineered wood floorings generally come pretreated with several layers of varnish and are ready for immediate use. Composite strips vary in thickness from 3/8 to 5/8 inch (9 to 15 mm). The strips can come in random lengths and be long (45 to 55 inches [120 to 140 cm]), short (10 to 20 inches [25 to 45 cm]), or as broad as 8 inches (20 cm). They are much less expensive than solid wood floorboards and are easy to install on top of tiles or bare concrete.

After 10 years or so, if the surface of the floor is slightly damaged, you may need to sand it to restore the original sheen.

Consider the following elements when choosing the flooring that best meets your needs: the type of wood (hard or soft), the thickness of the boards or surface layer, the treatment and finish, and the exact use of the floor. For rooms that will have a lot of foot traffic (entrances, hallways, or family rooms), opt for a solid wood floor in birch, chestnut, or walnut with a varnished finish. For rooms where the traffic is less intense (bedrooms), select an engineered wood floor with an ordinary pine surface.

For rooms that are subject to humidity (bathrooms and kitchens), choose a hardwood, such as teak, iroko, ipe, or jatoba, with a wax finish. To waterproof these woods more thoroughly, treat them with a varnish.

Right:

Terracotta floor
tiles and wooden
floorboards blend to
create a fine-looking,
natural, and thoroughly
country-style floor.

[Laying Tips]

Wood is one of the easiest floors to install. When laying hardwood or laminate flooring, it is important to allow it to adjust first to the room temperature and humidity. Do not accept delivery of wood on a wet day. Once it is delivered, acclimate the wood to the environment by leaving it in the room where it will be installed for five days prior to installation. If you are nailing down the wood strips, consider renting a flooring nailer. Lay down the first row, then, before continuing, lay out the remaining boards in the order that you will install them—pros call this "racking the boards."

[Bamboo]

Even though it grows with astonishing speed, making it one of the most renewable building materials, bamboo is made of naturally hard, stable, long, and tight fibers. It functions in the same way that hardwood does, with a very light, bright tone and smooth finish. It may be waxed or varnished, as desired.

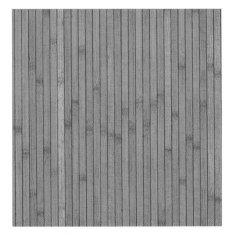

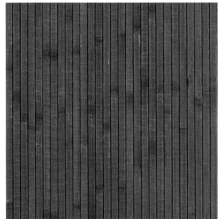

Above, right, and below:

One of the key properties of wood flooring is its capacity to take color while retaining the look of its grain and knots.

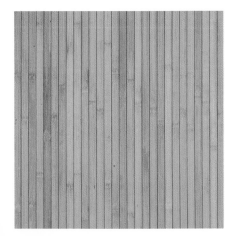

Finishes

Whether the floorboards are treated at the factory or are delivered in their original rough state, the choice of finish is crucial. After all, it is the finish that will determine the way the wood looks and the manner in which it must be maintained. Wax gives a rustic appearance and patina; oil preserves the natural, matte surface; and varnish, the hardest-wearing treatment, comes in matte, semi-gloss, or gloss finish and slightly darkens the material.

Coloring Wood

You can color wood and still leave its grain showing by using water-based wood stains (for soft woods such as pine) or spirit-based wood stains (which is better for hardwoods). The various shades available include dark oak, light oak, chestnut, and mahogany, among others. There is a drawback, however: Scratches and stains can be very visible, and difficult to hide, on a tinted wood floor.

Bleached Wood

After the surface of the wood has been sanded, it is bleached by impregnating it with a solution of a polymeric resin whitening agent. This type of treatment highlights the natural knots in the wood and is especially effective with wood varieties that have prominent features like oak, ash, elm, and chestnut. Follow the bleaching treatment—which can be achieved with varnish, whitening wax, or special paint—with a layer of varnish to protect the floor.

Paint

Paint can be applied to floorboards in such a way as to mask all of the wood's imperfections. Many different kinds of paint are available in a wide range of colors. The surface of the floor should be prepared and primed to make it smooth and non-absorbent, and then two coats of wood paint should be applied, allowing plenty of time for complete drying before the floor is used.

Wax

Wax is normally applied to bare wood after it has been sanded with an electric sander. The coating consists, quite simply, of a hard wax polish. Do not use a silicone-based product if you plan on applying varnish to the surface. Note also that a traditional wax finish, with its inimitable luster and fragrance, will require

Above:
Bleaching allows the grain of the wood to show to its best advantage.

Varnishing

frequent polishing and cleaning in future years, and is highly vulnerable to water. To make things easy for yourself, use a wax polish that cleans as it waxes.

Oil

Oil treatment gives wood a natural, satiny appearance, even though it is likely to darken the original color to some extent. In general, the oil-impregnation process is done in the factory and will make the wood highly resistant to stains, scratches, and abrasions. Maintenance is easy; dust can be removed with a broom or a vacuum cleaner, with an occasional thorough cleaning using a rejuvenating oil-and-water mixture applied with a clean cloth. For maximum shine, apply wax once or twice a year.

Varnish is by far the hardest-wearing finish and the one that causes the least problems. Once you have applied the treatment, you can forget about it for 10 years. Varnish protects against stains and general wear and tear, while showing off the grain of the wood to maximum advantage. A varnished floor is as easy to maintain as a tile floor, and whatever finish you choose—matte, gloss, or semi-gloss—you only need to dust from time to time, finishing off with a damp cloth.

Varnishing must be done on a dry, even, sanded, and dust-free surface. If the wood is new and untreated, work in good light so that you can quickly see areas where the product is too thickly or too thinly applied. When the first application has dried, rub the surface with a medium-grit sandpaper to improve the adherence of the second coat. If the wood is already varnished, a single coat will suffice, provided you have removed the protective polish and thoroughly cleaned the surface. Remember to focus on areas that are very worn, like doorways. Apply the product with a broad, flat brush.

Three Types of Varnishes

Polyurethanes—ready-to-use, if you are a beginner, or double-component, if you know what you are doing—take a long time to dry and have a very strong smell when wet. Moreover, the tools you use for the application are generally rendered useless for future projects. Yet these products are highly resistant to abrasion, scratching, and denting and are clearly the best for areas of heavy traffic in the house.

Acrylics, by contrast, dry rapidly and are odorless, plus your brushes can be washed in water and used again. Because they are not as durable as polyurethanes, acrylics are best suited to areas that are used less often. One advantage of acrylics is that you will not have to strip the entire floor should you ever need to renovate its surface.

Water-based varnishes have no smell, are nontoxic, and are environmentally friendly. They also dry very rapidly and work well for bedrooms.

[Soundproofing Wooden Floors]

However you lay the floor, it's best to install subflooring 1/8 to 1/4 inch (2 to 8 mm) thick between the floor and the new wood, as soundproofing. This underlayer, which can be polyethylene or mineral or vegetable fiber, will effectively muffle the noise of footsteps and increase your all-round comfort. Polyurethane foam, also found as a soundproofing underlayer, is known to be harmful to the environment.

Above:

To increase the sense of space, try using the same wood flooring in several contiguous rooms of the house.

Above:

Whether you use it for floors, walls, or ceilings, wood is guaranteed to bring naturalness and warmth to any room in the house.

Laying Techniques

Nailing down a wood floor is an exacting and expensive operation that requires a certain amount of professional skill. It should not be attempted in a room where the floor is liable to get wet or in a room where there is underfloor heating. It is, however, the right choice for traditional flooring laid on joists, beams, or false floors.

Gluing is ideal for thinner hardwood flooring laid on a flat concrete surface that is undamaged. It is recommended for humid rooms and can be used in rooms with underfloor heating.

The laminate type is best suited to thin—6 inch (15 cm) maximum thickness—hardwood floors and engineered wood. In this case, the strips are put together without gluing them to the floor; instead they are glued together along the grooves where they fit together. Stability results from the weight of the assembled mass. Laminate flooring can easily be assembled by amateurs on just about any floor, even if it is rough or is already covered with some other flooring material (such as vinyl, tiles, or stone), provided it is dry. Even more user-friendly are glueless snap-together systems called floating floors, which sit on a foam base and are held in place by their own weight.

Paneling

Wood enables us to live in an environment that is both natural and comfortable from a thermal and acoustic standpoint. It works well for walls, ceilings, and even foundations, and comes in a variety of species, widths, thicknesses, and finishes. For example, decorative wood paneling can be installed using pre-assembled wood elements. In remodeling, paneling can be very effective for hiding an imperfect wall surface, pipes, or electrical wires. Wood panels are available in a variety of timber species and finishes.

Laminate panels are considerably cheaper. They come in colors or in wood tones and are recommended for bathrooms and kitchens.

Solid pine boards are very popular, although they face stiff competition from oak, chestnut, wild cherry, walnut, and the various exotic woods, notably in a bleached finish that leaves the grain exposed. These boards tend to be varnished and tinted at the factory and come on the market ready-to-use. They require no subsequent treatment and can be used in any room in the house.

Painted Wood

Bare boards always require some kind of surface treatment; they should be waxed, varnished, or tinted with a product specific to the type of room and usage of the surface. For bathrooms, you can use the same kind of product recommended for weatherproofing wood outside—one adapted for rain, frost, and extreme temperatures.

Installing Paneling

The prep work and on-the-spot varnishing that used to be necessary for panel installation made it a laborious and costly process, best done by professionals. Today, most of the treatment and preparation is done at the factory, and simple tongue-and-groove edges are used for fixing the boards in place—so anyone can do the work. Boards can be arranged vertically, horizontally, or even diagonally. They are fixed to a framework that creates a space between them and the wall, allowing air to circulate freely. The framework is nailed to the wall, and is made up of laths that are 1 inch (25 mm) wide, ¾ inch (20 mm) thick, and approximately 15 to 25 inches (40 to 60 cm) apart. These ensure that the result is flat and level.

Insulation

To further improve insulation (given that wood is itself a natural insulating material), you may wish to install insulating material (fiberglass, polystyrene, hemp, or recycled denim) between the wall and the wood. Be sure to leave space for air to circulate; ventilation is especially important in bathrooms and other humid areas.

If you use wood for a bathtub surround, leave a space of 1 inch (25 mm) between the board ends and the floor, to prevent them being in prolonged contact with water. The boards may also be treated with linseed oil, which is a natural waterproofer, though it may darken the wood somewhat.

Boards may be laid out in several different ways depending on the decorative effect you desire. They can be installed vertically, horizontally, diagonally, or in a herringbone pattern—in attics, for example—or aligned with the lighting when used on ceilings. Note that a vertical pattern will emphasize the height of a room and diminish its length, while a horizontal pattern will emphasize depth and diminish height. A diagonal design, on the other hand, will create a sense of movement and flux. By juxtaposing boards of different lengths, you can produce a patchwork effect. And you may even want to add a personal touch to your panel work by using two different species of wood or two tints of the same species.

Wood Certification

If you use new hardwood, turn to the Forest Stewardship Council (FSC) to ensure reliable, widely honored certification. It will guarantee that the wood has been tracked from a certified managed forest to the finished product, and has followed sound sustainable steps along the way.

[**Wood** Treatments]

It is best to treat wooden boards with insecticide to eliminate any vermin that may attack them. Moreover, if there are any signs of humidity in your wall, treat the boards with a combination insecticide-fungicide, and attach them to a wood frame to keep them from being in direct contact with the wall.

Wood outside the House

On a balcony or terrace, you can screen yourself from prying eyes or protect yourself from the wind using an opaque latticework of wood, which is also an excellent floor covering for outside, in the form of wood grating, wooden paving, or outside floorboards.

Modular wood decking can come in square, rectangular, or hexagonal tiles generally made up of parallel boards screwed or clamped to joists with space in between to let water through.

Wooden paving consists of original blocks stapled to a plastic support for easy installation.

Outside floorboards, with spacing in between for rain runoff, offer an elegant alternative. Make sure the strips are evenly cut on both sides with planed or chamfered ends and angles so you don't get splinters in your bare feet. The ideal outside board should also be grooved so you don't slip on it when it's wet.

Popular species for outside are cedar, redwood, and southern yellow pine, but be aware of "exotic" woods that are often endangered. Not unlike recycled plastic, which is waterproof and eco-friendly, composite decking is more carefree than regular wood and can be found holding environmental labels.

Above:
Wood can be used as the floor for a terrace, provided a rot-resistant and dense species is used.

[**Laminate** Floors]

Developed in the late 1980s by a Swedish company, Perstorp, the laminate floor is a remarkable innovation. It consists of several materials assembled under high pressure: a protective layer of transparent synthetic resin, a laminated layer that covers decorative paper imitating wood, and a final layer designed to resist warping and keep the floor absolutely flat.

A High-Tech Solution

Laminate floors are highly versatile in that they have the appearance and warmth of real wood, while offering original, contemporary, even avant-garde effects. They are easy to lay and maintain, and at the same time astonishingly robust and hardwearing. With the exception of bathrooms (laminate floors don't do well in humid areas), they can be used for any room in the house. The extreme thinness of this product—¼ to ⅜ inch (7 to 10 mm)—makes it easy to install on just about any surface (tiles, boards, and the like). It can also be used to replace a carpet or vinyl floor without raising the floor level.

Laminate flooring has considerable technical advantages: It resists scratching, scoring, denting, and abrasion very efficiently and is unaffected by ultraviolet rays, stains, and cigarette burns.

Its ease of maintenance, above all, makes it extremely attractive—vacuum the laminate floor, then wipe it with a damp cloth, and it is clean. A word of caution, however: Never wet mop a laminate floor, and remove ordinary stains with a dry cloth only. More stubborn marks like ink, wax, or nail polish can be removed using an acetone solution, white spirit, or rubbing alcohol. Another amazing quality of laminate flooring is its tolerance for chlorine bleaches, which gives it the advantage of perfect hygiene.

Disadvantages: Unlike a classic wooden floor surface, you can't rejuvenate laminate flooring by sanding it, nor can you use wax, varnish, paint, soap, or abrasive powders for that purpose.

Advantages: Some of the new generation of laminates can easily be used with the latest underfloor heating techniques. Make sure this is specified on the label.

Laminates offer a wide range of selections to match any décor, with excellent imitations of wood species and intense colors for contemporary interiors. They perfectly reproduce all types of white, brown and red woods (such as beech, ash, oak, maple, walnut, and cherry) as well as stone varieties (such marble, granite, and slate) with exactly the right texture (such as knots, knurls, and roughness).

Their supreme quality, however, lies in their creative breadth, which encompasses all kinds of contrasting colors, material effects, and motifs. For example, using colored or imitation stainless steel aligned in strips as an outline to a single-tone surface creates a novel design.

Preceding pages:
Floors made up of different wood species have become fashionable, admired for their heightened decorative effects.

Right and below:
Mixing wood species offers floors that are more rhythmic and less monotonous than standard hardwood floors but just as warm and welcoming.

Cork

Cork, which is very light and durable, is made from the bark of the cork oak, broken up and dissolved in an oven with no chemical additives. Thus it is an entirely natural product. An excellent insulating material, it is also highly resilient, and its ocher and earth tints are very popular for modern interiors. It comes in squares, slabs, rolls, or planks, among other formats, and can be used for floors or walls. Cork has even been marketed with a strengthening layer of vinyl, which makes it waterproof. This covering should not be used with an under-floor heating system.

Cork is relatively inexpensive, and its lightness makes it easy to cut and lay. Nevertheless, it is best to unpack the cork tiles and lay them out flat for 48 hours before putting them in place, at which time they should be glued to a dry, flat surface.

Covering a Wall with Cork

Suspend a plumb line down the exact center of the wall and draw a vertical line beside it. Then draw a central lateral line using a set square or a level. Divide the wall into four equal zones, which you will then cover individually. Begin at the place where the lines cross. Apply glue to the first zone on the wall with a spatula or trowel and wait until it begins to harden, then place the first square exactly within the lines. Note that once the square is in place, it is impossible to adjust its position. Apply the next square in the same way, and repeat until all four zones have been covered.

Cork can be cut out with a ruler and cutter. For more complex cuts, take exact measurements or draw an outline on cardboard or paper to use as a template on the cork.

Laying Cork on the Floor

Divide the floor into four exactly equal zones and outline them with chalk. For complex cuts, as with wall cork, take exact measurements or draw an outline on cardboard or paper to use as a template on the cork.

Left, above, and opposite: Whether it is pale, brown, painted, or red, wood remains an incomparable material for creating an elegant and refined atmosphere.

Tile

Tiles are being offered in an ever-widening array of materials, formats, colors, and designs. With a touch of **imagination**, you can vary your décor and give every room in the house its own **distinctive character** by using tiles, whether solid-colored or patterned, traditional or contemporary.

Large tiles go with large rooms; for smaller spaces, use smaller tiles. Small tiles can quickly become monotonous, so don't hesitate to juxtapose different sizes of the same tile, or play with different laying techniques.

Putting up **wall tiles** is easier than laying **floor tiles**, but if you aren't sure of your skill as a handyman, you may prefer to use self-adhesive tiles. For large areas, opt for ready-made mosaics or panels of tiles, which will save you a great deal of time.

For a kitchen floor, avoid using plain white or even very pale tiles. The slightest smear will be painfully noticeable, and shoes will leave marks anytime there is water on the floor.

Above all, select tiles that go with the overall style of the room. Certain distributors offer complimentary decoration advice: A specialist is likely to suggest solutions that might not otherwise have occurred to you and may spare you from an expensive design mistake. On the Web sites of the major home improvement stores, it is possible to work up room-by-room simulations before you actually commit yourself to buying tiles.

Ceramic Tiles

Made of clay that has been fired with a glaze, ceramic tiles, which are available in deep, warm colors, offer a broad palette of creative possibilities. For example, you can combine bright tones with arabesque or intertwining flower motifs, with friezes, or with checkerboard patterns. Known for their durability and slightly rough surfaces, these tiles were widely used in the early 20th century and are making a real comeback.

Cement Tiles

Composed of a mixture of cement, sand, and marble powder, cement tiles are colored on one side only, then dried naturally, without firing. There are myriad collections of cement tiles with cabochons, friezes, and a variety of formats, which allow you to create your own personal décors in entrances, living rooms, kitchens, and bathrooms.

Cement tiles will last forever if they are properly laid. They can be mopped with soap and water, but should never be cleaned with anything stronger, such as acid or bleach.

Mosaic Tiles

Technically, the term *mosaic* refers to compositions made with tiles of enamel, stone, or glass measuring approximately ⅜ by ⅜ inch (9 by 9 mm). Mosaic brings color and texture to floors, walls, basin-surrounds, and other surfaces. The technique for covering any kind of surface with mosaic tiles, although time-consuming, is by no means as difficult as you might imagine. Using your own creative impulses, the process is very simple: All you have to do is patiently apply the small pieces of enamel, stone, or glass to wet mortar.

[Glass Tiles]

The transparency of glass has a sparkle all its own. Commonly manufactured using cast and fused glass methods, glass tiles are very hardwearing if properly set. Their tones are often redolent of the sea (indigo blue, watery green, turquoise, and the like), so they go well in bathrooms. But their durability and rich chromatic variety also make them appropriate for kitchens. As a floor covering, glass tile is best confined to areas where there is minimal traffic.

Make the mortar by mixing 3 parts cement and 2 parts water, and blending with a water-based glue, like EVA glue (2 parts water to 1 part glue), until it is a thick paste. Cover the surface with a layer of this mixture ¾ inch (20 mm) thick.

With a stick, draw the pattern you wish to create (choose a simple design to begin with) directly on top of the mortar. Place your mosaic tiles according to the design. Some pieces may need to be shaped, so have a tile saw or scorer handy. Allow the mortar to dry for about 24 hours.

Mosaic installation has become much simpler with the introduction of mesh-mounted mosaic sheets. These sheets are made up of mosaic tiles already placed in a design pattern (or made to appear randomly placed) on ready-to-use mesh grids. They are available in many home improvement stores and can be placed just like tiles, but with less effort, to create an overall design. This technique allows you to decorate even irregular-shaped areas easily and has an infinite number of uses.

Above and opposite:
Mosaic tiles make it possible to cover all sorts of surfaces, giving free rein to your imagination. Whether made of glass, stone, or ceramic, mosaic tiles are a material of choice for bathrooms and kitchens.

[**Encaustic** Tiles]

Encaustic or inlaid tiles are ceramic tiles made up of different colors of clay to create a pattern or figure on the surface. Highly decorative, they range from two to as many as six colors and may be glazed or unglazed. The pattern is inlaid into the body of the tile, so that the design remains even if the tile becomes worn down. The inlay may be imprinted from ⅛ inch to ¼ inch (2 to 8 mm) deep. Examples of encaustic tile floors are found all over Europe and the United States but are most prevalent in England, where the largest variety of inlaid tiles are made.

Right and below:

There are infinite ways of creating mosaics using repetitive or random patterns, different sizes of tile, friezes, or abstract motifs.

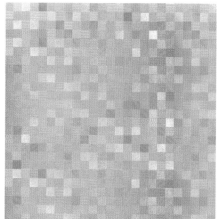

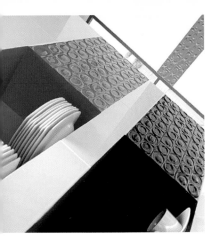

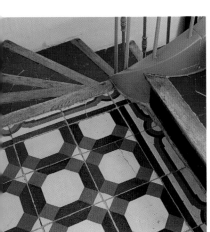

Above and right:

Tiles in relief, checker-
board patterns, rectangu-
lar tiles with acid colors,
encaustic tiles, tiles used
as trim—every room has
its own style of tiling.

Terracotta tiles are sold in different formats, shapes, and surfaces as squares, bars, hexagons, octagons, rectangles, shells, and so on. In the kitchen, 5-by-5-inch (12-by-12-cm) or 4-by-4-inch (10-by-10-cm) tiles are probably the most appropriate. Standard terracotta tiles come in ⅝ or ¾ inch (15 or 20 mm) thickness; they also come in a thinner ⅜ inch (9 mm) style, which can be used to overlay older tiles.

Three Types of Terracotta

Tiles handmade in the time-honored way offer much more variation than commercially made tiles. The tiles are thick and often irregular in shape, which gives them a charm of their own.

Machine-made tiles, commonly called quarry tiles, are much thinner and more regular but tend to be harder and more durable.

Terracotta

Timeless and inviting, terracotta is also wonderfully decorative. It is actually dried clay fired to a temperature of 1,650°F (900°C). Porous and unrefined at the outset, it becomes progressively more attractive as it acquires a patina.

Little maintenance is required for terracotta, which is impervious to heat or cleaning products. A month after it has been installed, you can make it fully resistant to water or grease by using a special spray. Allow it to dry

thoroughly before you walk on the tiles. To obtain an immediate shine, you can apply a satiny wax, but thereafter you will have to maintain the floor as if it were made of wood.

Even within the same color range each terracotta tile will have its own distinctive nuances, giving a textured look to any area, large or small. Before you lay the tiles, mix together the pieces from various boxes so the variations are uniformly distributed throughout the area.

Glazed terracotta offers a much wider range of uses than unglazed terracotta. It is far more resistant to wear and considerably less porous, and is therefore very popular for covering kitchen walls.

The color of terracotta tiles depends on the clay used to make them. Lighter ones blended with slate are more popular than the old-fashioned reddish color, which comes from the high iron oxide level in the source clay.

94

Opposite and above:

Terracotta increases in beauty and warmth as it acquires a patina over time.

1

2

3

4

5

Stoneware Tiles

Modern stoneware tiles are strong, durable, and resistant to frost and come in a wide range of colors suitable for contemporary floors. They are made from clay that is extracted from the earth, flattened, vitrified, cut, and single-fired at very high temperatures—at which time they become practically indestructible. They are also waterproof and stain-resistant, and their color will not alter even when subjected to regular direct sunlight. They can be found in every shade of earthy colors as well as in tones from gray to tender green to very soft blues. Their maximum size is 24 inches (60 cm) square.

Earthenware tiles are less regular, with unequal thicknesses and rougher edges, but they are every bit as robust as stoneware. Both resemble marble or natural stone when given a coat of colored glaze (matte, semigloss, or shiny). Glazed earthenware tiles can add a touch of color to work surfaces and kitchen walls.

Opposite:

Stoneware (1, 4, and 5) and porcelain (3) tiles are robust, waterproof, simple to maintain, and thoroughly decorative. The wide range of tiles available today in designs that reproduce the surface aspects of other materials, such as knots in wood (2), or the softness of fabric (5), can make tile floors look astonishingly alive.

[**Putting Up** Wall Tiles]

Installing wall tiles is much easier than installing floor tiles and is well within the capabilities of the amateur. First, check that the wall is perfectly even and flat, using a straight edge and a level. If the wall is painted, scrub and sand it to improve adherence. An older layer of tiles is also a perfectly good support, provided it is properly degreased. In this case, take care to use larger or smaller tiles than the originals for the new covering, so that the new joints never fall exactly over the old ones.

Always begin at the base of the wall. With decorated tiles, where the pattern is the most important thing, begin at one corner. Your choice of glue will depend on the nature of the surface, so follow the manufacturer's instructions with care. Self-adhesive tiles, which are very easy to install, save lots of time.

A tip for keeping tiles shiny: Rub them from time to time with half a lemon, cut side down, then wipe them off with a dry cloth.

Opposite:

Playful, brightly colored, subtle, or contemporary, wall tiles are frequently sold in panels, which allows them to be installed much more quickly.

Right and below:

Black-and-white tile designs have been popular for centuries, and they remain so in modern-day applications.

1

2

3

4

Above:

Materials can have a strong impact or influence on design. Like indestructible steel plates, glazed stoneware tiles (2 and 3) transform the floors and walls into vibrant surfaces. Other designs use alternate colors for tiles on different surfaces (1 and 4), while an even more complex style in a bathroom project (4) includes a subtle weave of colored stripes—all done with glazed stoneware tiles.

Above:

Renovations that include
re-covering surfaces and
organizing space afford
welcome opportunities
to explore new combina-
tions of colors and
materials. The latest
generation of tiles is rich
in fresh possibilities.

Porcelain Tiles

The most exposed areas of any kitch-
en are behind the sink, the stove,
and the counter. Natural, porous
terracotta is unsuitable for these
spaces, but porcelain tiles, which
are too fragile for floors, are perfect because they are impervious to
stains, detergents, and the ravages
of time. Hard-wearing, waterproof,
and easy to maintain, porcelain tiles
are also much prized for their decorative value.

Porcelain tiles are available in a wide
variety of colors and motifs, with
matte or shiny, smooth or rough finishes. You can enhance a two-color
décor, for example, by accentuating

[**Kitchen** Countertop]

Kitchen work surfaces receive a lot wear and tear—scrapes and drips, hot pans, water, detergents. They have to be durable as well as good looking. Surfaces covered in tiles, mosaic, or porcelain are especially effective in these types of conditions.

The tiling technique for a horizontal work surface is very similar to that used for walls, except that the joints are slightly different. Tiles on these surfaces must be applied with a rubber tool and rise to the exact level of the tiles on either side so that they do not accumulate dirt and bacteria in between. Choose a water- and mold-resistant filler that is durable enough to stand up to frequent scrubbings with harsh products like bleach, the mortal enemy of mold and germs. If you need to cut more than a half-dozen of the tiles to make them fit, you will save time if you buy a tile cutter.

Below:

In this kitchen, dark gray stoneware and red decorated porcelain tiles are not only practical but also extremely attractive.

Above:

Glazed stoneware tiles
offer a perfect imitation
of stone's characteristic
unevenness.

it with a decorative frieze of porcelain tile. In bathrooms, the new generation of glazed tiles can imitate raw materials as different as stone, earth, and cement, making it possible to create attractive décor easily and at relatively little cost.

Moreover, this material is well suited to areas that are exposed to water; walls covered in glazed porcelain tile will remain impeccable for many years, provided the joints are regularly maintained.

Stone

Natural stone, with its delicate veins and subtle shades, has an inimitable beauty. Stone tile enhances every kind of city décor, contemporary or otherwise, as well as houses in the country. A few hard or very hard types of stone are suitable for floors and can be a substitute for wooden floors or wall-to-wall carpeting. Their surfaces can be smooth, textured, or polished like marble.

Marble

Marble is the most prized and luxurious calcareous stone in existence. There are more than a hundred varieties, with all manner of beautiful veins and grains. Marble comes in several formats, notably square or rectangular tiles, in a variety of sizes from 1 inch (6 cm) square to 20 inches (129 cm) square, and different thicknesses, from ¼ inch (8 mm) to 1¼ inches (3 cm). The thinner tiles are easier to install and are equally good for floors and walls. Shapes like trapezoids and hexagons are also available.

Slate

Using slate, with its various lovely tones of gray, you can create a floor that is virtually indestructible (short of hitting it with a sledgehammer). Slate has other benefits, too: It is resistant to fading and to stains and is generally nonslip. If it is thin enough, it can be installed just like ordinary tile.

Granite

Granite is an unalterable type of stone, and the finer its grain the harder it will be. It is sold in a number of different forms, notably matte, polished, and shiny. Shiny finishes are well-loved because they show off the beauty of granite's very fine veins.

Sandstone

Sandstone and limestone may be more brittle than other tiles but they are an economical alternative, offering a brilliant variation on natural stone that is suitable for both interior and exterior applications.

Maintaining Stone

As a basic protection for a stone floor, you can brush on a coat of a special waterproofing solution. This will leave a durable, stain-resistant, chemical-resistant, and nonslip protective film.

Opposite:

A breathtaking imitation of broad marble flagstones reinforces the overall impression of openness and space.

Left and opposite:
Frosted glass and
glass blocks safeguard
privacy in these bath-
rooms while allowing
light to filter through.

[Glass]

When an area of the house does not have any windows, glass partitions and floors can help compensate for the lack of natural light. Glass blocks, which are strong enough for load-bearing walls, also have sound- and heat-insulating properties. Using glass for partitions can divide a space without cutting off any existing light. The transparency of a glass-tile floor can also relay natural illumination from a skylight down through to the lower levels of a house.

[**Glass Tiles** and Blocks]

Glass tiles are excellent insulators when they are double-glazed (you can also use hollow ones), and they are specially designed for floors. In general, they are assembled with reinforced cement mortar at least 1¼ inches (3 cm) thick. Glass blocks, by contrast, offer a satisfactory solution in situations where light is required but not necessarily transparency. They have the same load-bearing qualities as brick and will efficiently transmit between 77 and 85 percent of the light that falls on them.

Resilient
Flooring

Resilient or synthetic flooring has become popular for use in every room of the house. Although it was once confined to kitchens and bathrooms, it has become much more attractive, with fresh new colors and patterns and textures that imitate natural materials and even metal surfaces with surprising accuracy. In fact, the designs have been refined to the point where it is sometimes hard to tell that the material is synthetic. This type of flooring is very **easily maintained**, is **extremely durable**, and comes in various finishes—all at very affordable prices.

An excellent member of the resilient flooring family, **linoleum** flooring is a composite material made of jute, linseed oil, cork, and resin melded together at high temperatures and glued to a jute or hemp fiber backing. It owes its name to the linseed oil that is one of its principal components, and it is entirely **biodegradable and recyclable**.

Invented in Great Britain during the 19th century, linoleum spread rapidly to other parts of the world during the 1920s. It fell out of favor after the Second World War, having acquired a reputation for dreariness, stiffness, and brittleness. Today, however, it has made a spectacular comeback for domestic use, having been significantly improved by new manufacturing methods. In its contemporary guise, it is not only very durable but also bacteria repellent, antistatic, UV resistant, and resistant to heel marks. As if this were not enough, when it comes with an underlayer of cork it has excellent soundproofing qualities.

Rubber flooring is the **most durable** and often used in high traffic areas or exercise rooms. It can be found in sheets or tiles, including convenient interlocking ones, and when bought recycled, it is eco-friendly.

Most **vinyl or PVC** flooring is now considered a hazard to the environment and people's health, from its manufacturing processes to its use and disposal. Many esteemed organizations, such as Greenpeace and Healthy Building Network (HBN), condemn this once-popular material.

[**Properties** of Vinyl and PVC]

Vinyl and PVC floors are resistant to wear and tear, water, and grease marks, but are vulnerable to cigarette burns and sudden temperature changes. They are virtually indestructible, washable, and rot-resistant and are an excellent solution for bathroom and kitchen floors that are likely to get wet.

Above:

Resilient flooring that imitates wide wooden floorboards fits naturally into this kitchen area.

Vinyl is a chameleon-like material: It can imitate anything from wood to stainless steel, stone, slate, terracotta, marble, and even pebbles. It is easy to install and maintain and is suitable for any room of the house, especially those where a natural material would be too fragile (like bathrooms and kitchens).

A vinyl floor that replicates, for example, teak or wenge wood (including natural-looking joints), works very well in a bathroom or kitchen without presenting the drawbacks of real hardwood flooring. For an equally convincing and decorative result, try a vinyl floor that looks like wood with a wide floorboard pattern. Very realistic representations of all kinds of wood species are available in this versatile material. Thanks to newly invented techniques for imitating wood grain, it can now resemble the real thing not only visually but also in terms of texture. Some patterns actually feel like they have real knots and veins of wood or the roughness of terracotta.

If they are backed with a substantial layer of high-density foam, vinyl floors have excellent acoustic properties. What's more, they are relatively soft underfoot, pleasant to walk on, and muffle footsteps. It is important, however, to be clear about the different qualities of vinyl. The thicker the underlayer, the better the floor's acoustic performance. In terms of durability and toughness, the thicker the surface layer that you walk on, the better. There are different quality classifications—durability under different conditions of use, as well as the levels of water resistance, punc- ture resistance, and resistance to chemicals—that will help you decide which vinyl best meets the requirements of your room.

As a general rule, in high-traffic areas such as hallways and entrances the surface layer will need to be 2.5 millimeters thick. A dining room or a child's bedroom calls for a thicknes of 2 millimeters, and other bedrooms and living rooms will require a thickness of 1.2 millimeters to 1.5 millimeters. In the bathroom, make sure the underlayer is thick enough to make for a floor that is soft and comfortable to walk on barefoot.

Composite vinyl is sold in the form of flexible sheets without an underlayer, and the color or pattern is dyed right through the material. It is highly durable and relatively cheap, but its

[**Easy** Maintenance]

Resilient flooring is hygienic and clean, thanks to the modern anti-stain and anti-bacteria treatments it undergoes during manufacturing. These surface treatments also help reduce porosity and make the floors easy to clean. Simply vacuum surface dust, then clean with soapy water and rinse. Stubborn stains can be removed with a cloth moistened with white spirit. A word of warning: Avoid using harsh cleaning products containing ammonia and solvents.

thinness makes it a very poor insulating material. Moreover, it must be laid perfectly flat and smooth to have any chance of lasting.

Solid vinyl, also called all-vinyl, is composed of vinyl pieces set in a vinyl base. This is sturdy and comfortable to walk on and is an excellent insulator. When combined with an underlayer of vinyl, cork, rubber, or polyester, its performance is even better.

The wear layer, a protective film, tops all vinyl flooring. It consists of either urethane, which is clear with no wax covering, or vitrified vinyl. The vinyl type, more resistant to stains and scratches, varies between 1.5 and 4 millimeters in thickness. Though its wear layer is transparent, it provides the vinyl's toughness, durability, and nonslip characteristics, protecting the printed and structured lower layer that provides the design, color, and texture.

An underlayer, which is usually made of fiberglass, is sometimes incorporated to add a solid dimensional stability to the overall flooring. A foam backing provides increased comfort and ensures excellent sound and heat insulation.

[How to Lay Synthetic Tiles]

Be sure to check the exact mode of installation before you buy tile. Some tiles need to be glued in place, usually with acrylic glue, while others are self-adhesive and can be repositioned, if necessary. There are also weighted tiles, which are held in place by their own weight.

Right and below:

Original designs and a range of interesting textures are now available thanks to modern techniques. The resemblance to wood and other natural materials can be both visual and tactile.

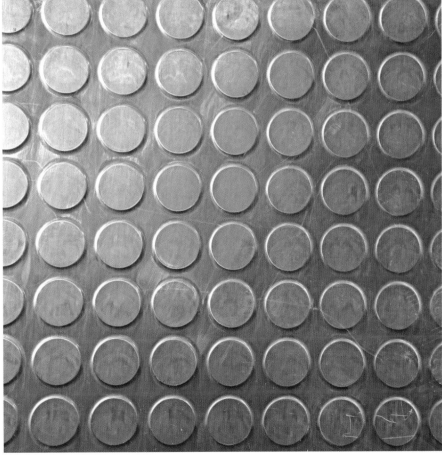

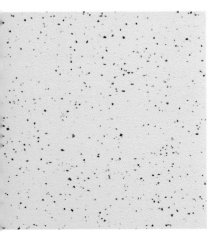

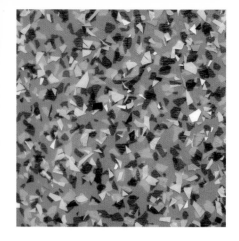

Synthetic Tiles

Vinyl flooring is also available in the form of tiles. In addition to being easy to handle and install, vinyl tiles greatly reduce the waste generated by cutting large pieces down to fit specific areas. But perhaps the greatest advantage of vinyl tiles is the fact that you can replace individual tiles as you need to; only the damaged piece needs to be removed, not the whole floor. Moreover, with tiles, you can easily and cheaply assemble a floor using colors and dimensions of your choice to create all sorts of patterns: checkerboard, herringbone, trompe l'oeil—anything is possible.

Rubber

Rubber is a common feature of public buildings, though it is less often used in homes. Rubber comes in a single color and usually has a nonslip surface. It stands up well to wear and tear, cigarette burns, and high heels, but it is vulnerable to many kinds of solvents and chemical cleaning products. It can be laid directly on a smooth, flat concrete surface, provided the corners are cut out carefully. To give it more durability, it can be coated with a water-emulsion finish. It is best cleaned with slightly soapy water. Ridged rubber floor coverings need to be regularly cleaned to prevent dust buildup.

Installing Resilient Flooring

Resilient flooring can be laid on just about any type of surface (concrete, cement, hardwood floor, tiles, and so on) provided it is in good condition.

First, strip your old tile surface, filling in gaps and smoothing the filler. The same goes for wooden floors, which should be stripped, then planed or sanded level, and reinforced, if necessary. Spaces between the boards should be filled in with a filler or wood putty. If the floors are severely damaged, they can be covered with a thin layer of plywood. Cement or concrete floors should be smoothed off and any holes carefully filled.

Unroll sheets at least 24 hours before you lay it. After the flooring is laid, wait a good 48 hours before moving in furniture. For rooms not exceeding 200 square feet (20 square meters), you can use double-sided adhesive tape, making it very simple and quick to put in place, following the contours of the floor covering.

For larger areas, try laying the flooring with no adhesive at all; heavy furniture will help to stabilize it completely.

Above:

Contrary to popular belief, linoleum is not a plastic product. Linoleum is a resilient floor covering made up of jute fibers

and the linseed oil that gives the material its name, and is also 100 percent recyclable.

Metal

Metal has become increasingly popular and is ubiquitous in contemporary city apartments. Rather than being concealed as they once were, metal surfaces and fixtures are instead being deliberately shown off.

Stainless steel is a blend of **steel**, **chrome**, and **nickel**. It will not warp, buckle, or corrode; is extremely durable; and lasts virtually forever. Stainless steel is also non-reactive, and will not affect food that comes into contact with it; this is why it is the preferred material of restaurant chefs and of the food industry in general.

Stainless steel was not as popular during the 1980s because of a general lack of creative products offered by manufacturers. But it has experienced a real resurgence in recent years, and is often paired with dark or light wood. It comes in three distinct finishes: **polished**, **brushed**, and **lightly textured**. The first is the most difficult to maintain, as it stains and scratches easily. The other two finishes are more durable. Stainless steel can achieve a patina over time, and although the first scratches will be annoying, the millions of others that follow will be of no consequence.

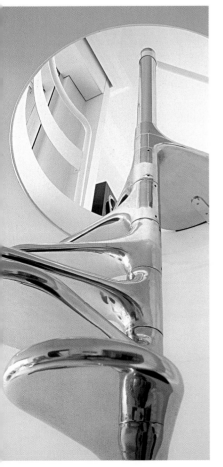

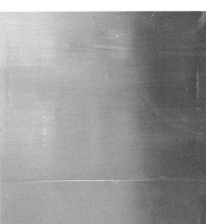

[**Metal:** Preparing the Support]

Using a putty knife, fill in all areas prone to rust with resin. Scrape off excess resin with the blade of the knife, or allow it to dry before smoothing it with sandpaper.

Preceding page:

Stainless steel

and metal feature

prominently in the

décor of many modern

apartments.

Opposite:

Metal and frosted

glass form a subtle yet

elegant decorative com-

position in a light-filled

apartment entrance.

Rust Treatment

To strip a small area of metal that has rusted, rub it well with sandpaper. Use a metal brush for larger surfaces that have begun to rust or are covered in peeling paint. For a very large metal surface, the easiest way to remove marks is by using a drill with a nylon brush attachment.

To remove rusting paint, brush on a thick coat of chemical paint stripper. When the paint has softened, use a toothbrush to remove it from all corners and crevices. Clean the metal with water or white spirit, and then apply a rustproofing product with a brush all over the surface.

Painting Metal

New metal paints consisting of an alkyd-urethane mix offer long-lasting, vibrant colors and a high level of protection against rust. They are resistant to nicks and scratches as well as to the expansion and contraction of the metal support. They can be applied directly, with no undercoat, to any iron or metal surface in good condition.

[**Maintaining** Stainless Steel]

Stainless steel can be maintained on a daily basis with a soapy sponge, and weekly with a stainless steel cleaner. If your water is high in calcium, you can remove deposits with rubbing alcohol or vinegar.

Below:
Beams, work
surfaces, storage,
and furniture—today,
metal is used for many
residential purposes.

Below and following spread:

Both hygienic and functional, stainless steel is very popular in kitchens, as well as other areas of the home.

Bibliography

Adams, Heather E. and Earl G., Jr. *Designing a Home with Wood.* New York: Stewart, Tabori & Chang, 2004.

———. *Stone: Designing Kitchens, Baths, and Interiors with Natural Stone.* New York: Stewart, Tabori & Chang, 2002.

———. *Tile Style: Creating Beautiful Kitchens, Baths, and Interiors with Tile.* New York: Stewart, Tabori & Chang, 2005.

Dubois Petroff, Marie-Pierre. *Recettes d'architecte: La salle de bains.* Paris: Charles Massin, 2000.

Carli, Félicien. *Le petit guide illustré de la chaux: comment faire? Des astuces, des recettes, les conseils d'un spécialiste.* Paris: Les Cahiers de Terre et Couleurs, 2001.

Cassell, Julian, Peter Parham, Mark Corke, and Mike Lawrence. *Repair and Renovate Your Home (DIY).* Sydney: Murdoch Books, 2003.

Caure, Hélène. *Bien décorer et aménager votre maison.* Paris: Solar, 2001.

Chabot, Pierre, Annie der Bedrossian, and Hervé Abbadie. *Paris: Maisons de ville.* Paris: Minerva, 2001.

Guild, Tricia, Elspeth Thompson, and James Merrell. *Inspiration.* London: Quadrille Publishing, 2006.

Hutchinson, Janetta. *Contemporary House.* Bath, U.K.: Parragon, 2002.

Kaldewei, Gerhard. *Linoleum: History, Design, Architecture, 1882–2000.* Ostfildern-Ruit, Germany: Hatje Cantz, 2000.

McCloud, Kevin. *Choosing Colors: An Expert Choice of the Best Colors to Use in Your Home.* New York: Watson-Guptill, 2003.

———. *Complete Book of Decorating Styles and Techniques.* London: Dorling Kindersley Publishers Ltd, 1990.

Miller, Judith. *Judith Miller's Color: Period and Regional Style from Around the World.* New York: Clarkson Potter, 2000.

Monahan, Patricia, and Trevor Dean. *Papier peint: Choisir son papier, bien s'équiper, tout préparer et nettoyer, tapisser du sol au plafond.* Paris: Marabout, 2005.

———. *Peinture, Choisir sa peinture, bien s'équiper, tout preparer et nettoyer, quelle technique employer.* Paris: Marabout, 2005.

Périphériques Architects. *Your House Now: 36 Propositions for a Home.* Basel, Switzerland: Birkhäuser, 2002.

Roberts, Meg and Steven. *Color at Home: Creating Style with Paint.* New York: Stewart, Tabori & Chang, 2008.

Steffen, Alex. *Worldchanging: A User's Guide for the 21st Century.* New York: Abrams, 2008

Sutton, Tina, and Bride M. Whelan. *The Complete Color Harmony: Expert Color Information for Professional Color Results.* Beverly, MA: Rockport Publishers, 2004.

ViaGardini, Iris. *Enduits et badigeons de chaux.* Paris: Editions Eyrolles, 2006.

Votre maison, Tout pour bien vivre chez soi. Paris: Larousse, 2005.

Willemin, Véronique. *Maisons vivantes.* Paris: Editions Alternatives, 2006.

Source List

Some of the more specialized materials discussed in this book may be difficult to find. Always try your local supply dealer first, then larger companies, many of which sell by mail order. Sources listed below are both local and international, but the list is by no means all-inclusive.

American Lime Technology (AMT) is a joint venture of U.K.-based Lime Technology Limited and U.S. Heritage Group, Inc., which is based in Chicago. AMT is the exclusive North American distributor of Hemcrete® construction materials.
Phone: +1.773.414.5486 (contact Bruce Petersen)
Email: info@americanlimetec.com
www.americanlimetec.com

APA: The Engineered Wood Association is the authoritative source for information on structural wood products and their related construction applications.
Phone: +1.253.565.6600
Email: help@apawood.org
www.apawood.org

Ariostea is an Italian company specializing in the manufacture of high-tech marble, stone, and wood.
Phone: +39.0536.816811
Email: info@ariostea.it
www.ariostea.it

Artesano is a full-service construction and consulting company located in Boulder County, Colorado, available for start-to-finish installation of natural building technologies that include earth plaster systems, lime plaster, and *tadelakt.*
Phone: +1.303.718.4932
Email: ryan@artesano-home.com
www.artesano-home.com

Atelier d'Offard is a small company in Tours, France, that specializes in traditional block-printed wallpapers and creates exact reproductions of antique originals as well as contemporary designs.
Phone: +33.2.47.67.93.22
Address: 9, rue Anatole-France, 37300 Joué-les-Tours, France

Atelier LZC designs and creates wallpaper and stickers.
Phone: +33.1.42.87.81.34
Email: celine@atelierlzc.fr (export contact: Céline Dupont)
www.atelierlzc.fr/accueil_gb

Benjamin Moore Paint has been producing high-quality paints and finishes since 1883 and delivers them directly to retail stores and dealers worldwide.
www.benjaminmoore.com

Bettencourt Green Building Supplies offers innovative products at affordable prices. Developed through research and experience, their new materials provide elegant and appropriate alternatives to many of the environmentally damaging choices currently available in the industry.
Phone: +1.718.218.6737 or +1.800.883.7005
Email: info@bettencourtwood.com
www.bettencourtwood.com

The **Carpet and Rug Institute** (CRI) is a source of extensive consumer information on carpets, and also tests and certifies carpets and carpet-cleaning products with their seal of approval and Green Label/Green Label Plus program.
Phone: +1.706.278.3176
Email: info@carpetrecovery.org
www.carpet-rug.org/residential-customers

Carpet America Recovery Effort (CARE) is a joint industry-government effort to increase the amount of recycling and reuse of post-consumer carpet, offering great suggestions and ideas for building materials.
www.carpetrecovery.org

Cléton in Pairs offers a variety of plasters, gilding materials and finishes, natural pigments, and specialized tools.
Phone: +33.1.47.00.10.41
Address: 41, rue Saint-Sabin, 75011 Paris
www.cleton.fr

Clipso Design creates both beautiful and utilitarian ceiling and wall coverings using their state-of-the-art stretch polyester material, which can be printed with solid colors, designs, or digital images; produced in dimensions up to 16 by 165 feet; and installed quickly and easily for seamless, maintenance-free surfaces.
Phone: +1.310.450.5727 and +41.26.460.5588
www.clipso-usa.com and www.clipso.ch

Compact Concrete, founded by Francesco Passaniti, uses innovative methods to create concrete for interior applications, including floors, walls, shelves, and furniture.
www.compactconcrete.com

Crucial Trading is a company with a passion for creative floor coverings in wool, jute, hemp, seagrass, sisal, and other natural materials; their products are found online and at retailers worldwide.
Phone: +44.845.076.0086
www.crucial-trading.com

Dalsouple makes rubber flooring in a wide range of gorgeous colors and textures for commercial and domestic use. Almost all of their products are available in DalNaturel natural rubber, an environmentally friendly and sustainable resilient flooring.
Phone: +44.1278.727.733
Email: info@dalsouple.com
www.dalsouple.com

Décor Tadelakt is a specialized plastering company with many years of experience, providing samples of *tadelakt,* customizing mix and match colors, and installing plaster finishes for projects around the world.
Phone: +44.7866.758.020
Email: info@tadelakt.co.uk
www.tadelakt.co.uk

Design by Color™ is available at participating decorating centers and paint and wallpaper retail stores in North America and offers more than 3,000 wallpaper options, designer tips on choosing and using patterns, and photos of inspiring color solutions.
Phone: +1.800.539.5399
Email: info@designbycolor.net
www.designbycolor.net

Designers Guild is one of the foremost international home and lifestyle companies designing, manufacturing, and distributing furnishing fabrics, wall coverings, and home accessories.
Phone: +44.20.7893.7400
Email: info@designersguild.com
www.designersguild.com

Demesne is a Web site dedicated to collecting and disseminating information about topics that concern homeowners, in a clear, simple format that demystifies what it takes to maintain and improve personal space.
www.demesne.info

DIYinfo.org is one of the many cost-free and independent, community-run information Web sites that anyone can edit or add to and share their knowledge of do-it-yourself projects.
www.diyinfo.org

DIYnetwork.com features broadband video channels focusing on home improvement and woodworking, along with step-by-step instructions for more than 20,000 projects online.
www.diynetwork.com

eCarpetProtection.com is a consumers' guide to carpets and carpet protection that provides information about caring for, cleaning, and purchasing carpets.
Email: cfreviews@earthlink.net
www.ecarpetprotection.com

Elitis of France makes outstanding wall covering and designer fabrics that are distributed around the world.
Phone: +33.1.45.51.51.00
Address: 35, rue de Bellechasse, 75007 Paris

Emery & Cie, founded by the architect Agnes Emery, offers paint and wall coatings, fine cloth, tiles, carpets, and wallpaper, among other interior design products.
Phone: +1.718.767.8218
Email: claude.emery@emeryetcie.com
www.emeryetcie.com/en

Farrow & Ball manufactures high-quality wallpapers and paint in colors of great depth and a full range of finishes.
Phone: +1.888.511.1121
Email: nasales@farrow-ball.com
www.farrow-ball.com

Forbo is a global leader in the production and marketing of linoleum-based floor coverings and hardwood flooring, as well as bonding materials for floors.
Phone: +1.866.Marmoleum (North America)
Email: info@themarmoleumstore.com
www.forbo-flooring.com

The Forest Stewardship Council (FSC), an international organization that helps to find solutions that promote responsible stewardship of the world's forests, administers a global forest management certification system that is recommended by environmental organizations, social groups, and businesses.
www.fsc.org/en

Habitat is a U.K.-based international home furnishings retailer with its own retail operations in the U.K., France, Spain, and Germany, in addition to a large distribution network of retail partners around the world.
Phone: +44.870.411.5501
Email: customer.relations@habitat.co.uk
www.habitat.net

The Hemp Industries Association (HIA) is a nonprofit trade group representing hemp companies, researchers, and supporters.
Phone: +1.707.874.3648
www.thehia.org

The Home Depot is the world's largest home improvement retailer, with stores throughout North America, Canada, Mexico, and China, as well as online.
www.homedepot.com

ICI Group is one of the world's largest decorative paint and coatings manufacturers, with operations in 55 countries.
In the United States: +1.800.984.5444
www.iciduluxpaints.com

Ikea, a Swedish-based company, offers a wide range of well-designed, functional home furnishing products at low prices in retail stores around the world.
www.ikea.com

In Création designs and creates personalized wall coverings using a digital file or sketch of an original concept, as well as offering designs from their catalog.
Phone: +33.1.49.29.09.45
Email: contact@increation-online.com
www.increation-online.com

Interface manufactures creative interior design materials such as modular carpet, broadloom carpet, and decorating fabrics.
www.interfaceinc.com

Kahrs manufactures hardwood floating floors that are easy to install; retailers are located worldwide.
Phone: +1.800.Ask.Kahrs (275.5247)
Email: Admin@kahrsstore.com
www.kahrs.com

Kvadrat develops high-quality modern textiles and textile-related products for both architects and private consumers.
Phone: +45.8953.1866
Email: kvadrat@kvadrat.dk
www.kvadrat.dk

Lafarge is one of the largest diversified suppliers of construction materials in the world, active in 76 countries. In North America, they produce and sell cement, ready-mixed concrete, gypsum wallboard, aggregates, asphalt, and related products and services.
www.lafarge.com and www.lafargenorthamerica.com

Le Dean Burrus Domestic Studio manufactures decorative wall coverings, including products using Ductal, a hyperfine concrete for both interior and exterior use.
Phone: +33.1.45.67.47.19
Address: 7, rue Bachaumont, 75002 Paris

Lelievre, a Paris-based company, is one of the leading international manufacturers and distributors of fine furnishing fabrics as well as interior accessories.
Phone: +33.1.43.16.88.00
Email: export@lelievre.eu
www.lelievre.eu

Mosaic House sells hand-made traditional Moroccan mosaic tiles, including mosaic ceramic, cement, hand-painted, and chiseled tiles that are suitable for walls, floors, and counters, in both interior and exterior installations.
Phone: +1.212.414.2525
Email: contactus@mosaichse.com
www.mosaichse.com

NALFA, formed by U.S. and Canadian manufacturers and importers of laminate flooring, has developed a certification system for tested and examined laminates to allow consumers to make sound purchasing decisions.
www.nalfa.com

Nora Rubber Flooring is a worldwide company creating top-quality rubber floor coverings that deliver enduring performance with inspired designs that allow for creativity.
Phone: +1.978.689.0530
Email: info@nora.com
www.norarubber.com

ThePaintStore.com offers a huge range of paints and painting supplies at wholesale prices.
Phone: +1.800.456.0966
www.thepaintstore.com

Perfectino coatings are designed according to the criteria of qualified craftsmen working closely with chemists. Products include *tadelakt,* stone, and a new Perfectino decorative finishing system developed for both the professional and do-it-yourselfer.
www.perfectino.be

Porcelanosa, a Spanish-based company, is a world leader in manufacturing wall and floor tiles in a wide range of sizes and finishes.
Phone: +34.901.100.201
Email: info@porcelanosa.com
www.porcelanosa.com

Sikkens provides a range of coating systems, including interior and exterior wall paint, translucent finishes and varnishes, fillers, products for metal protection, lacquers, and products for maintaining and repairing concrete.
Phone: +31.71.308.2809
www.sikkens.com

Italiantiles.com provides links to other institutional Web sites that feature information on ceramic tiles of Italy, including manufacturers, importers, design trends, promotional activities, and events around the world.
www.italiantiles.com

Rubber-Cal offers a complete line of rubber matting and flooring that includes green and recycled products for virtually any application, providing a cost-effective, warm, resilient, and durable alternative to hard and cold surfacing.
Phone: +1.714.772-3000 or
+1.800.370.9152
Email: customerservice@rubbercal.com
www.rubbercal.com

Sto develops products, systems, and services for building projects throughout the world based on a concept that combines aesthetic and functional diversity with environmental awareness.
www.sto.com

Tarkett is one of the largest producers and distributors of resilient flooring and hardwood flooring in the world.
www.tarkett.com

The **Tile Heritage Foundation**, founded in 1987 as a nonprofit organization, is dedicated to promoting awareness and appreciation of ceramic surfaces in the United States.
Phone: +1.707.431.84.53
www.tileheritage.org

Tile of Spain is a trade association listing all Spanish tile manufacturers and new trends in tile designs.
www.spaintiles.info

Valentino Decorative Plaster provides specialty interior and exterior decorative finishes that add classic beauty to any wall. Valentino has a full line of acrylic-based and lime-based finishes, including *tadelakt*.
Phone: +1.800.600.6634 or
+1.951.737.7447
Email: info@omega-products.com
http://valentino.omega-products.com

Vénilia has created a full range of matching products, including decorative adhesives and friezes, to help provide imaginative decorating solutions for any interior space.
www.venilia.fr

Vetrazzo's artful surfaces are strong, durable, and made of 85 percent recycled glass.
Phone: +1.510.234.5550
Email: info@vetrazzo.com
www.vetrazzo.com

Walldesign, a French company, produces easy-to-use "objects to make" (rather than "ready-made products") that involve the consumer in the creative process of home decoration.
Phone: +33.1.43.48.30.24
Email: contact@walldesign.fr
www.walldesign.fr

Wallpapers Plus offers great prices on an outstanding selection of wallpapers, stickers, and stencils.
Phone: +1.888.242.7448
Email: customerservice
@wallpapersplus.com
www.wallpapersplus.com

Acknowledgments

Francesca Torre and Olivier Hallot would like to give their warm thanks to those who contributed to the realization of this book: Marie-France de Saint-Félix, Vania Nalin, Marcio Uehara, Gilles Bouchez, Muriel Lagneau, Annie Verlant, Jean-Jacques Ory, Dominique Mey, Francesco Passaniti, Stéphane Zamfirescu, Céline Carbonel, Simonetta Greggio, and René Kormann.

Francesca Torre would like to give special thanks to the designers and manufacturers whose work enriched the illustrations in this book.

Photographic credits

All photographs are the work of Olivier Hallot, except:

Concrete: Passaniti Francesco: p. 9 (nos. 2, 3, 4, 6, 9, 11, and 12); p. 10; p. 12 (all images); p.13 (no. 1); p. 15 (nos. 1, 2, 3, and 4). Le Dean Burrus Domestic Studio: p. 10 (no. 5), p. 15 (no. 5). BathShop: p. 9 (no. 10); p. 13 (no. 2).
Limewash: Marie-France de Saint-Félix: p. 19 (no. 3); p. 20.
Paint: Emery & Cie: p. 27 (nos. 1, 4, 6, and 8); p. 31 (no. 1); p. 32; p. 33; p. 35 (nos. 3 and 5); p. 38; p. 39. Tollens: p. 27 (no. 5); p. 28; p. 34; p. 35 (no. 4); p. 36; p. 37 (all images). Dulux Valentine: p. 30 (no. 2); p. 31 (no. 4). Annie Verlant: p. 30 (no. 1). Robert le Héros: p. 35 (no. 1).
Wallpaper: Atelier LZC: p. 41 (no. 1); p. 47. In Création: p. 6; p. 41 (nos. 2 and 3); p. 42 (nos. 1 and 2); p. 43 (nos. 1, 2, and 3); p. 44–45; p. 48 (nos. 1, 2, 3, 4, 5, and 6); p. 49 (nos. 1, 2, 3).
Wall Fabric: Lelievre: p. 51 (nos. 1 and 2); p. 53 (nos. 2 and 4). Tassinari & Chatel: p. 51 (no. 3). Descamps: p. 53 (nos. 1 and 3).
Carpet: Toulemonde-Bochart: p. 55 (nos. 4, 6, and 7); p. 57; p. 59 (nos. 1, 2, 3, 4, and 5); p. 60; p. 61; p. 62 (no. 1). Robert le Héros for Tarkett: p. 55 (no. 2) . Saint-Maclou: p. 55 (nos. 1 and 3); p. 62 (nos. 2 and 3). Emery & Cie: p. 56. Décorasol: p. 55 (no. 5).
Wood: Kahrs: pp. 80–81; p. 83 (nos. 1, 2, and 3); p. 84 (no. 3); p. 85. Porcelanosa: p. 84 (nos. 1 and 2).
Tile: Emery & Cie: p. 87 (no. 1); p. 88. Surface: p. 87 (no. 2); p. 92 (nos. 2 and 3); p. 99 (no. 2). Diagonale: p. 87 (nos. 3, 4, 5, 7, 10, 11, and 12); p. 92 (no. 4); p. 99 (no. 2); p. 100 (nos. 2, 3, and 4); p. 104 (nos. 3, 4, 5, and 6); p. 105. Lapeyre La Maison: p. 87 (no. 6); p. 92 (nos. 5 and 6); p. 93 (no. 3); p. 102 (nos. 1 and 2). Tiles of Spain: p. 87 (no. 9); p. 90; p. 93 (no. 1); p. 96 (nos. 1, 2, 3, and 4); p. 98 (nos. 1 and 3); p. 99 (nos. 1 and 3); p. 100 (no. 1); p. 101 (no. 1); p. 103; p. 104 (nos.1 and 2); p. 106; p. 107 (no. 1).
Resilient Flooring: Forbo Sarlino: p. 109 (all images); p. 110; p. 112; p. 114 (all images); p. 115. Décorasol: p. 113 (nos. 3, 4, and 5).
Cover: Bathshop (image); In Création (left edge design).

Published in 2008 by Stewart, Tabori & Chang
An imprint of Harry N. Abrams, Inc.

Copyright © 2007 by Aubanel, an imprint of Editions Minerva, Geneva, Switzerland
English translation copyright © 2008 by Stewart, Tabori & Chang, New York

Library of Congress Cataloging-in-Publication Data
Torre, Francesca.
  [Materiaux. English]
  Materials : a sourcebook for walls and floors / by Francesca Torre ;
  [translated from the French by Anthony Roberts].
    p. cm.
  Includes bibliographical references.
  ISBN 978-1-58479-726-5
  1. Flooring. 2. Wall coverings. 3. Interior decoration—Materials. 4. Dwellings—
Maintenance and repair. I. Title.
  TH2525.T67 2008
  747—dc22
                    2008022782

Book design: Séverine Morizet

Translated from the French by Anthony Roberts

Editor, English-language edition: Magali Veillon
Designer, English-language edition: Shawn Dahl
Production Manager, English-language edition: Jules Thomson

The text of this book was composed in Officina Sans, Officina Serif, and Helvetica Neue.

Printed and bound in Spain
10 9 8 7 6 5 4 3 2 1

HNA
harry n. abrams, inc.
a subsidiary of La Martinière Groupe

115 West 18th Street
New York, NY 10011
www.hnabooks.com